The Broader Implications of Ericksonian Therapy

Ericksonian Monographs

The Broader Implications of Ericksonian Therapy

Edited by Stephen R. Lankton

Brunner/Mazel Publishers • New York

Library of Congress Cataloging-in-Publication Data

The broader implications of Ericksonian therapy / edited by Stephen R. Lankton.
    p.   cm. — (Ericksonian monographs : no. 7)
    Includes bibliographical references.
    ISBN 0-87630-582-6
    1. Hypnotism—Therapeutic use.   2. Psychotherapy.   3. Erickson, Milton H.   I. Lankton, Stephen R.   II. Series.
    [DNLM: 1. Erickson, Milton H.   2. Hypnosis.   3. Psychotherapy. W1 ER44 no. 7 / WM 415 B863]
RC495.B74   1990
616.89'14—dc20
DNLM/DLC
for Library of Congress
                                89-71310
                                CIP

Published by
BRUNNER/MAZEL, INC.
19 Union Square
New York, NY 10003

Manufactured in the United States of America

10 9 8 7 6 5 4 3 2 1

Ericksonian Monographs

Ericksonian Monographs publishes only original manuscripts dealing with Ericksonian approaches to hypnosis, family therapy, and psychotherapy, including techniques, case studies, research and theory.

The *Monographs* will publish only those articles of highest quality that foster the growth and development of the Ericksonian approach and exemplify an original contribution to the fields of physical and mental health. In keeping with the purpose of the *Monographs*, articles should be prepared so that they are readable to a heterogeneous audience of professionals in psychology, medicine, social work, dentistry and related clinical fields.

Publication of the *Ericksonian Monographs* shall be on an irregular basis; no more than three times per year. The Monographs are a numbered, periodical publication. Dates of publication are determined by the quantity of high quality articles accepted by the Editorial Board and the Board of Directors of the Milton H. Erickson Foundation, Inc., rather than calendar dates.

Manuscripts should be submitted in quintuplicate (5 copies) with a 100–150-word abstract to Stephen R. Lankton, M.S.W., P.O. Box 958, Gulf Breeze, Florida 32562-0958. Manuscripts of length ranging from 15 to 100 typed double-spaced pages will be considered for publication. Submitted manuscripts cannot be returned to authors. Authors with telecommunication capability may presubmit one copy electronically at 2400, 1200 or 300 baud rate and the following communication parameters: 8 bit word size, No parity, 1 stop bit, x-on/x-off enabled, ASCII and xmodem transfer protocols are acceptable. Modem times are 7p.m. – 7a.m. CST on 904-932-3118.

Style and format of submitted manuscripts must adhere to instructions described in the *Publication Manual of the American Psychological Association* (3rd edition, 1983). The manuscripts will be returned for revision if reference citations, preparation of tables and figures, manuscript format, avoidance of sexist language, copyright permission for cited material, title page style, etc. do not conform to the *Manual*.

Copyright ownership must be transferred to the Milton H. Erickson Foundation, Inc., if your manuscript is accepted for publication. The Editor's acceptance letter will include a form explaining copyright release, ownership and privileges.

Indexing will include both name and keyword references. When submitting a paper, please list key words, key concepts and all names cited. These will be referenced across all papers so be judicious about choices, and do not include Dr. Erickson.

Reference citations should be scrutinized with special care to credit originality and avoid plagiarism. Referenced material should be carefully checked by the author prior to first submission of the manuscript.

Charts and photographs accompanying the manuscripts must be presented in camera-ready form.

Copy editing and galley proofs will be sent to the authors for revisions. Manuscripts must be submitted in clearly written, acceptable, scholarly English. Neither the Editor nor the Publisher is responsible for correcting errors of spelling and grammar: the manuscript, after acceptance, should be immediately ready for publication. Authors should understand there will be a charge passed on to them by the Publisher for revision of galleys.

Prescreening and review procedures for articles is outlined below. Priority is given to those articles which conform to the designated theme for the upcoming *Monographs*. All manuscripts will be prescreened, absented of the author's name, by the Editor or one member of the Editorial Board and one member of either the Continuing Medical Education Committee or the Board of Directors of the Milton H. Erickson Foundation, Inc.

Final acceptance of all articles is done at the discretion of the Board of Directors of the Milton H. Erickson Foundation, Inc. Their decisions will be made after acceptable prescreened articles have been reviewed and edited by a minimum of four persons: two Editorial Board members, one member of the CME Committee or the Board of Directors, and the Editor. Occasionally, reviewers selected by the Editor will assist in compiling feedback to authors.

Feedback for authors and manuscript revision will be handled by the Editor usually between one and two months after submission of the prepared manuscript. Additional inquiries are welcomed if addressed to the Editor.

Contents

Articles

Contributors

Richard Fisch, M.D.
  Private practice; Clinical Associate Professor of Psychiatry, Stanford; and Research Associate, Principal Investigator, and Director, Brief Therapy Center, Mental Research Institute, Palo Alto, California.

Douglas G. Flemons, Ph.D.
  Assistant Professor of Family Therapy, Institute for Systemic Therapy, Nova University, Ft. Lauderdale, Florida.

John C. Gall, M.D.
  Pediatric practice, Ann Arbor, Michigan.

Stephen G. Gilligan, Ph.D.
  Private practice, San Diego, California.

Bradford P. Keeney, Ph.D.
  Professor, Counseling Psychology, College of St. Thomas, St. Paul, Minnesota, and Institute for Systemic Therapy, Nova University, Ft. Lauderdale, Florida.

William J. Matthews, Ph.D.
  Associate Professor, Counseling Psychology Program, School of Education, University of Massachusetts, Amherst, Massachusetts.

William R. Nugent, Ph.D.
  Human Resource Development and Training Director, Florida Network of Youth and Family Services, Tallahassee, Florida.

Akira Otani, Ed.D.
Staff Psychologist, University of Maryland Counseling Center, College Park, Maryland, and parttime Faculty, Johns Hopkins University, School of Continuing Studies, Baltimore, Maryland.

Robert E. Pearson, M.D.
  Private practice, Houston, Texas.

Ernest L. Rossi, Ph.D.
  Clinical psychologist in private practice, Malibu, California; editor of the *Collected Works of Milton H. Erickson on Hypnosis;* editor of *Psychological Perspectives,* a semiannual journal of Jungian thought.

Steve de Shazer, M.S.S.W.
  Director of the Brief Family Therapy Center, Milwaukee, Wisconsin.

Introduction

This issue features a dialogue among acknowledged experts concerned with the influence of the work of Milton H. Erickson, M.D. Most readers of the Ericksonian Monographs will be familiar with the far-reaching impact of Erickson's contribution. Indeed, beginning in 1952, the Gregory Bateson "Schizophrenia Project" and later the Mental Research Institute (MRI), both based in Palo Alto, studied Erickson's work as it departed from traditional therapy. Erickson's communication-based approach offered, perhaps for the first time, a nonpathological orientation toward treating human suffering. For instance, as early as 1955 Gregory Bateson proposed that Erickson's therapeutic binds in hypnosis (Bateson, 1972a, p. 223) and in waking state (Bateson et al., 1968, p. 50) demonstrated that hallucinations were a way a family member could resolve contradictory communications.

Several major departures from the conventional epistemology of psychotherapy were articulated by Bateson and his associates between 1952 and 1974. For example, Bateson explicated the understanding that "feelings" are "patterns of relationship" (Bateson, 1972b, p. 140), that events in smaller [individual] contexts must always be considered as part of a larger [family/social] context (Bateson, 1972c, p. 246), and that control of any behavior—problem or otherwise—is to be found spread through-out a family system and not merely in an individual "self" (Bateson, 1974d, pp. 313–320). These are but three of the numerous restatements of fundamental underpinnings of therapy made by Bateson and his associates during years of intensive and regular study of Erickson's work. The full impact of these understandings has yet to be realized in the therapy field. Members of MRI, including Paul Watzlawick, John Weakland, and Richard Fisch, have worked to apply these concepts clinically.

Contained in this volume is a position paper by Richard Fisch, M.D., in which he states his views about what Erickson's work *can* become and what he hopes it will *not* become in the future. Fisch is well qualified to cast judgment in these matters since his 1962 membership in the Family Training Committee of the Mental Research Institute provided a wealth of contact with Bateson, Haley, Jackson, Weakland, Watzlawick, and most certainly, the methods of Milton Erickson. Since 1965 Fisch has been a Research Associate, Principal Investigator, and Director of the Brief Therapy Center at MRI. He has authored and co-authored several books and articles, including *Tactics of Change—Doing Therapy Briefly* and *Change—Principles of Problem Formation and Problem Resolution*. It was in this later book that the concept of "reframing" was best clarified and illustrated. Erickson wrote the introduction for the book. It is with confidence, then, that we turned to Fisch for his thoughts about the evolution of Erickson's influence. His response is entitled "The Broader Implications of Milton H. Erickson's Work."

Following Fisch's article are eight rejoinders from experts representing a diverse range of theory and practice. The list includes brief therapist Steve de Shazer, M.S.S.W.; researchers and clinicians William J. Matthews, Ph.D., and William R. Nugent, Ph.D.; hypnotherapist Stephen G. Gilligan, Ph.D.; family therapists and theorists Bradford P. Keeney, Ph.D., and Douglas G. Flemons, Ph.D.; psychiatrist and long-time friend of Erickson, Robert E. Pearson, M.D.; and Jungian analyst and Erickson's co-author and frequent collaborator, Ernest L. Rossi, Ph.D.

Understandably, there is difference of opinion in each of these articles. Readers will discover that this diversity of conviction tells a story that is, perhaps, *the* broader implication of Erickson's work.

This issue also includes representative articles about the continuing research and application of Ericksonian ideas. From the research of Akira Otani, Ph.D., at Johns Hopkins, we have "Structural Characteristics and Thematic Patterns of Interspersal Techniques of Milton H. Erickson: A Quantitative Analysis of the Case of Joe." Otani's analysis suggests some major advantages in using interspersal techniques as well as general guidelines for their clinical implementation.

The timely research by William R. Nugent, Ph.D., from the Florida Network of Youth and Family Services, entitled "An Experimental and Qualitative Evaluation of an Ericksonian Hypnotic Intervention for Family Relationship Problems," demonstrates that hypnosis may be a useful change-inducing method for family therapy.

In the area of application, all therapists working with children will find a wealth of ideas on naturalistic utilization in the chapter "The Art of Examining a Child: Uses of Naturalistic Methods in the Pediatric Physical Examination," by an eminent private practice pediatrician, John C. Gall, M.D.

This volume of *Ericksonian Monographs* is thought provoking and

provides practical ideas for a wide readership. We hope that the conversations begun here will continue to spur debate, dialogue, research,
and developments in clinical practice.

STEPHEN R. LANKTON,
Gulf Breeze, FL
April 1989

References

Bateson, G. (1972a). Toward a theory of schizophrenia. In *Steps to an ecology of mind: A revolutionary approach to man's understanding of himself* (pp. 201–242). New York: Ballantine Books.

Bateson, G. (1972b). Grace, style, and information in primitive art. In *Steps to an ecology of mind: A revolutionary approach to man's understanding of himself* (pp. 128–152). New York: Ballantine Books.

Bateson, G. (1972c). Minimal requirements for a theory of schizophrenia. In *Steps to an ecology of mind: A revolutionary approach to man's understanding of himself* (pp. 244–270). New York: Ballantine Books.

Bateson, G. (1972d). The cybernetics of 'self.' In *Steps to an ecology of mind: A revolutionary approach to man's understanding of himself* (pp. 309–337). New York: Ballantine Books.

Bateson, G., Jackson, D., Haley, J., & Weakland, J. (1968). Toward a theory of schizophrenia. In D. Jackson (Ed.), *Communication, family, and marriage: Human communication* (Vol. 1, pp. 31–54). Palo Alto: Science and Behavior Books.

The Broader
Implications of
Ericksonian
Therapy

The Broader Implications of Milton H. Erickson's Work

Richard Fisch, M.D.

This paper argues that Milton H. Erickson's work demonstrated a conceptual shift. The major importance of his work concerns the removal of the implication of pathology and his knowing use of interpersonal influence; his major contributions were not his developments in hypnosis or his definition of the unconscious. However, in the dissemination of Erickson's ideas, professionals often fail to build on these important contributions and instead focus on elaborations of his technique. As a result, a possibility for the development of new ideas and approaches for solving personal, interpersonal, and social problems is missed. Although Erickson's work is a major departure from the traditional, it is feared that his work will be remembered as simply another of a number of "therapies" rather than as a paradigmatic shift in the field of mental health.

The purpose of a position paper is to promote dialogue about what is happening in the field of therapy, not to impart new information. Hopefully, the animated discussion generated by this and subsequent position papers can clarify issues in our field and stimulate new ideas.

Let me state my position at the outset: It is my concern that in the dissemination of Erickson's ideas, professionals fail to build on the *conceptual* doorways implicit in his work and instead focus on emulations or elaborations of what might be called his "technique." As a result, opportunities will be missed for the development of new ideas and approaches for solving personal, interpersonal, and social problems. At risk is the compartmentalizing of his work as simply one of a number of "therapies"; thus the title of this position paper.

In explaining my position, let me offer some historical perspective. All ages and all cultures have had their own beliefs about human problems

Address correspondence to: Richard Fisch, M.D. Director, Brief Therapy Center, Mental Research Institute, 555 Middlefield Rd., Palo Alto, CA 94301 and have designated people to deal with those problems. These people have been called shamans, priests, seers, witch-doctors, physicians, psychotherapists, and so forth. But, I believe, the term "change agents" is a useful generic application.

Cultural beliefs about the nature of problems determine the way change agents deal with them. If what the change agents do "works" enough of the time, their beliefs about problems come to be regarded as truth. Beliefs, conceptualizations, or models vary enormously both in their particulars and in their relative simplicity or complexity. For example, it is surmised that prehistoric humans had very simple notions about deviant behavior. Since they appeared to practice trephaning, it is assumed that they explained problems on the basis of pressure or spirits entrapped within the skull. Logically, then, releasing whatever was entrapped should correct the individual's deviance. In contrast, contemporary psychoanalysts would have a much more complex explanation (or model), one involving a progression of life experiences creating an intricate interplay of forces influencing the "mind" and, therefore, the behavior of the individual.

While these and all other models developed through the ages differ from each other, for the most part they share the idea that there is something wrong, defective, or missing within the individual or, as in current family therapy concepts, that there is something wrong or "dysfunctional" within the family system. That is, models traditionally revolve around some notion of pathology and the notion that such pathology has to be eradicated, modified, or nullified through understanding (or, "insight") in order to alter deviant behavior. However, inherent in much of Erickson's work is a departure from this notion, and his depathologizing of human problems represents an important "doorway." This was a remarkable step, evolving as it did in an era that was and continues to be dominated by the belief that problems stem from diseases of the mind, namely, "mental illness."

In his explanations of his work and, more so, in descriptions of his work itself, Erickson regarded problems as unremarkable ("normal") striving by the individual for independence, pleasure, or meaning—striving that had become painfully stalemated, however. Mainly, he tried to get people "unstuck." His approach was not limited to certain types of problems; every kind of problem came his way, from people acting "crazy" to kids acting up. For the most part, Erickson got his patients to *do* things. Some tasks were simple, some complicated; some were novel and humorous; some were arduous. But, with few exceptions, they were incorporated within everyday and mainstream activities.

Erickson did not do things that implied pathology. He did not rely on medication or hospitalization, nor did he ask patients to dwell on or confess to shameful events in their lives. When improvement occurred, he didn't have his patients linger on in protracted "termination" from therapy. Also, in the arduousness of many of his tasks, he indicated a disbelief in the fragility of patients. His focus was mainly on getting people to redirect their striving and, thereby, get over the stumbling blocks in their lives. One cannot do all of these things without operating on the notion that there isn't much if anything wrong with the "patient." Thus Erickson depathologized and, concomitantly, demystified human problems.

Erickson also opened up another doorway: He studied communication from the standpoint of influencing change. In particular, he employed linguistics and paralinguistics therapeutically. Historically, the influence of change agents was limited to consensually accepted rituals and the acceptance of the change agent's authority or "power" within the culture. Usually change agents did not need much more than that to fulfill their role and function. Usually directives were not all that were conveyed by change agents—something additional was conveyed indirectly. The priest, for example, was presumed to serve as a communicational conduit between the spirit of god and the deviant, or the "afflicted"; the task or ordeal prescribed did not "really" come from the priests. But the range and sophistication of indirection was markedly limited and often stereotyped.

The advent of hypnosis led to increasing sophistication in the use of indirection. Much of it began with Mesmer's ideas of "animal magnetism" in the eighteenth century. In attempting to influence people, Mesmer believed it necessary to use a fairly ritualized procedure resulting in a type of behavioral response later labeled as "trance." It was and still is presumed that in "trance," the "subject" is in an altered state of suggestibility, consciousness, or responsiveness. For the most part, hypnotists still rely on some ritualized practice, theatrical or simple, to produce the response in another defined as "trance." Erickson redefined the "altered state" as one of an expanded awareness of possibilities and options. But his retention of the notion of an altered state—a "trance" state—is consistent with his thinking of problems from a monadic, or individual-oriented, viewpoint. (Contrast his view with that of Haley, who defines hypnosis as a communicational exchange or interaction between hypnotist and subject, 1973, p. 20.)

Nevertheless, within his framework about hypnosis, Erickson evolved a study of how people responded to him and to each other. Concomitantly, he undertook a disciplined study of the use of verbal and nonverbal communication to alter responses and, ultimately, problem behavior. (One might say that "talking therapy" began with hypnosis, but until Erickson, speech was not regarded as an influential and potent tool all by itself.) In evolving his linguistic approach, whether he used metaphors, analogies, innuendo, contradiction, "trance," or just plain "talk," Erickson opened the doorway to investigating and refining *concepts* of interpersonal influence.

It is my opinion that Erickson's developments in "hypnosis" are not the major, or potentially major, impact of his work; nor of major importance is his redefinition of the "unconscious" as benign and creative (actually Jung's conception of a benign unconscious preceded Erickson's). Rather, the *context* or *concept* of "trance" allowed Erickson to develop a discipline of human influence, and the *metaphor* of "unconscious" as benign gave him the freedom to depathologize human problems.

My concern is that these two bridges to the development of more effective ways of resolving human problems will be obscured and not crossed. Too much interest in Erickson's work has been shunted into replications of his hypnotic technique and vocabulary (Kershaw, 1987; Matthews, 1987; Rossi, 1987). Reification of his use of the "unconscious" metaphor will, likewise, cloud the fullest implications of a depathologized view about problems. If one reviews much of the new "Ericksonian" literature (e.g., the Ericksonian Monographs and the proceedings of the various Congresses held in Phoenix), it seems that his work has come to mean all things to all people, representing diverse models, yet without any apparent change in any of those models. One operates on the notion that problems are a reflection of some sort of underlying pathology or that they are not. Representatives of several models, including psychoanalytic, Rogerian, behaviorist (Gunnison, 1987; Allen, 1987; Leveton, 1982; Cohen, 1982), have adapted Erickson's techniques to their models without altering the basic ways they view problems.

I commented above that Erickson was monadically oriented (Haley, 1973, p. 95), and I know this must sound strange to many readers. He often did work with family members of the patient and talked about family life and the relationship of the patient's problem to members of the family. Nevertheless, in his work, he focused on the identified patient; work with family members tended to be ancillary to that principal focus. No matter how difficult or "resistant" the patient was, Erickson still tended to work with him or her rather than with the broader social context of the family. Using this focus, Erickson developed more and more effective means of influencing people. That development has even greater potential, however, and I have already commented on that. The point I am raising here is that, reverence for Erickson's accomplishments aside, it would limit the expansion of ideas not to reexamine and challenge his monadic viewpoint. And, as I have also commented, the reification of "the unconscious" will limit the expansion of Erickson's seminal contributions by keeping them from being integrated into another conceptual "revolution"—that of systems concepts.

Finally, I am concerned that emphasis on such things as hypnotic techniques and "addressing the patient's unconscious" will tend to make treatments longer, not shorter, as is often the case when treatments are mysterious. Unfortunately, there seems to be an attraction to the elaborate and mysterious. My hope, of course, is that we will be free to examine and challenge ideas and techniques, even Erickson's, so that we can build on his daring and important contributions.

References

Allen, J. (1987). The self and its survival in the work of Milton Erickson. In S. Lankton (Ed.), *Central themes and underlying principles* (Ericksonian Monographs, 2, pp. 40–55). New York: Brunner/Mazel.

Cohen, S. B. (1982). Erickson's techniques and psychoanalysis. In J. Zeig (Ed.), *Ericksonian approaches to hypnosis and psychotherapy* (pp. 173–180). New York: Brunner/Mazel.

Gunnison, H. (1987). Comparison of values and beliefs of Milton H. Erickson's utilization approach with C. R. Rogers' person-centered approach. In S. Lankton (Ed.), *Central themes and underlying principles* (Ericksonian Monographs, 2, pp. 15–29). New York: Brunner/Mazel.

Haley, J. (1973). *Uncommon therapy: The psychiatric techniques of Milton H. Erickson, M.D.* New York: Norton.

Kershaw, C. (1987). Therapeutic metaphor in the treatment of childhood asthma: A systemic approach. In S. Lankton (Ed.), *Central themes and underlying principles* (Ericksonian Monographs, 2, pp. 83–95). New York: Brunner/Mazel.

Leveton, A. (1982). Family treatment as play: the contribution of Milton H. Erickson, M.D. In J. Zeig (Ed.), *Ericksonian approaches to hypnosis and psychotherapy* (pp. 201–213). New York: Brunner/Mazel.

Matthews, W. J. (1987). Hypnotherapy with chronic pain: An ecosystemic approach. In S. Lankton (Ed.), *Central themes and underlying principles* (Ericksonian Monographs, 2, pp. 69–82). New York: Brunner/Mazel.

Rossi, E. L. (1987). Memory and hallucination (Part II): Updating classical association theory to a state-dependent theory of therapeutic hypnosis. In S. Lankton (Ed.), *Central themes and underlying principles* (Ericksonian Monographs, 2, pp. 32–39). New York: Brunner/Mazel.

Erickson's Systemic Perspective

Steve de Shazer, M.S.S.W.

In principle, I am reluctant to comment on someone's comment on anything, but I am particularly reluctant to comment on someone's comment on Erickson's work because I am averse to Erickson's deification, a process that leads to disputes about "who is more Ericksonian," "who is more correctly Ericksonian," etc. These haggles are akin to medieval ones about "how many angels can dance on the head of a pin" and therefore are, at best, not very useful and, at worst, confuse and befuddle us, leading us away from what is important.

However, I have a long-held respect for Dick Fisch. He does not talk (or write) very much, but when he does, it is worth listening to (or reading); therefore, I will overcome my reluctance.

Fisch has clearly stated his position, which might not be too popular with some "family therapists" and less so with some so-called Ericksonians. I could not agree with Fisch more: It is seductively easy to become infatuated by the wonderful variety of trance inductions, metaphors, stories, etc., and thus lose sight of Erickson's paradigmatic revolution. The foundation of that revolution involves the underlying patterns of his work rather than the specific applications, or techniques, based on those patterns. This is not to say that technique is trivial or unimportant. Far from it. It might not be going too far to say that, when it comes to *doing* therapy, technique is all there is to the therapist's part of the conversation. But technique is based on the underlying ideas about the job at hand (namely, theory), and Erickson's ideas were uniquely systemic, although their systemic nature remained more or less tacit.

Erickson's revolution primarily concerned how therapists think about or see their job (their world view). Fisch and I are on the same track here. As I see it, Erickson seems not to see pathology, just everyday human problems, and to define his job as influencing change.

Address correspondence to: Steve de Shazer, Brief Family Therapy Center, 6815 W. Capitol Drive, Milwaukee, WI 53216.

Influence, as Fisch uses the term in describing Erickson's work, is a systemic idea. The job of a therapist is to influence the client. There must be someone who is influencing someone else, and there must be something for the receiver of influence to be influenced about, or the term is vacuous. Fisch states this idea rather elegantly. (So far, so good. Commenting on a comment has not produced any difficulties.)

The difficulty begins.   Which brings me to the point where my view or construction differs from Fisch's. Both are, unfortunately, re-views of Erickson's view. Both might be similar to Erickson's view; both might be totally dissimilar; one might be similar and the other not. Unfortunately, Erickson is not around to set us straight. But it is important not to be confused: The comparison here is really between Fisch's view or construction and my view and the potential pertinence of either or both. We are not bickering over "who is more Ericksonian." Remember: Neither is necessarily Erickson's view nor even necessarily similar to Erickson's view. They are not comments on Erickson's view.

Fisch views Erickson's work as *monadically* oriented* and therefore not working with the family-as-a-system. As I see it, Erickson was profoundly systemic, but the system he gave consideration was not "the family system," but "the therapy system." Minimally, this is a *triadic orientation:*

1) patient plus
2) therapist plus
3) the problem they are jointly working on solving.

Without this problem-solving task, it is just a conversation, nothing more. This conception is, of course, tacit in Fisch's emphasis on the influencing aspect of the therapist's job.

By abstracting more or less formal patterns from Erickson's work (de Shazer, 1978, 1979, 1982, 1985, 1988), it is clear that he was a great generalizer. When what he and the client were doing reminded him of some previous case (or story), he frequently used that memory as a model. The model and the current example might be radically different in terms of problem or symptom or age or marital status or stage of life or the number of people concerned, but this did not matter. His ability to compare disparate examples is part of his genius and suggests that comparison between systemic patterns involving the therapist-client-problem system is useful in doing creative therapy. This is exactly *not* a monadic view of the individual. A monadic view ultimately leads back to

---

*"Monad" is usually defined as an ultimate unit, as something simple, and implies a self-sufficiency and a lack of connection to other units.

individual pathology, which, I believe, is not Fisch's view at all, and it certainly was not Erickson's.

Conclusion

The difficulty resolved.   This leaves us with an unfortunate either/or construction: either Fisch's view or my view. It might be simplest to leave it at that, but this kind of construction is the root of my reluctance. Instead, using Erickson's method of putting disparate examples together allows for a both/and construction that might be useful.

It seems clear that Fisch and I would agree that Erickson was not a family therapist—if by that term one means a view that defines the therapist's job as including insisting on seeing the whole family and some-how changing the family because there is something wrong with the family system (sometimes in order to solve the problem). Rather, Erickson seems to have been interested in using his influence to change the *systemic* relationship between his patient (usually an individual, but it could be a couple or a family) and the patient's problem. Erickson's therapy did not depend at all upon the number of people he was talking to. The "client unit" (Fisch's monadic orientation) was just one element of the system under consideration (namely, a second element in my triadic orientation, and the therapist-as-influencer completes the triad).

References

de Shazer, S. (1978). Brief hypnotherapy of two sexual dysfunctions: The crystal ball technique. *American Journal of Clinical Hypnosis, 20*(3), 203–208.

de Shazer, S. (1979). On transforming symptoms: An approach to an Ericksonian procedure. *American Journal of Clinical Hypnosis, 22*, 17–28.

de Shazer, S. (1982). *Patterns of brief family therapy.* New York: Guilford.

de Shazer, S. (1985). *Keys to solution in brief therapy.* New York: Norton.

de Shazer, S. (1988). *Clues: Investigating solutions in brief therapy.* New York: Norton.

In Defense of Hypnosis

Stephen G. Gilligan, Ph.D.

Richard Fisch's major contention seems to be that "depathologized views" and "interpersonal influence" are the "twin towers" around which Milton Erickson's contributions may be advanced. Fisch correctly points out that "change agents" through the years have viewed problematic behavior primarily in terms of some hypothesized defect ("badness or madness"), and that Erickson demonstrated a major paradigmatic shift by conceptualizing such expressions as normal, albeit rigid, developmental behavior. Rather than focusing on past difficulties that needed to be explained or eliminated, Erickson oriented to future possibilities that could be achieved. In doing so, he framed complaints within a nonpathological context of developmental strivings. I agree with Fisch's assertions that this constitutes a fundamental shift in approaching therapy and that therapists will be severely limited if they attempt to use Erickson's techniques without also making this fundamental shift.

I also agree with Fisch's suggestion that Erickson's emphasis on the role of interpersonal influence in stimulating change is another major contribution that has been underdeveloped. Being intensely committed to promoting change, Erickson explored many avenues by which his communications could influence patients positively. In doing so, he developed a therapeutic approach that requires therapists to be active, directive, and extremely flexible in their communications. By claiming that therapists have a responsibility to actively influence clients to promote change, Erickson differed fundamentally from traditional approaches. And as Fisch correctly argues, this critical difference has often been neglected or undervalued by those attempting to build on Erickson's work.

While Fisch acknowledges Erickson's sensitivity to interpersonal influence, he also respectfully criticizes what he terms Erickson's

Address correspondence to: Stephen G. Gilligan, Ph.D., 1504 Crest Drive, Encinitas, CA 92024.

"monadic" viewpoint—orienting primarily to individuals (rather than, presumably, to recursive interpersonal relationships. While I agree that a pure "monadic" viewpoint is unnecessarily limiting and probably outdated, this may not be the best characterization of how Erickson operated. As Fisch points out, Erickson frequently made use of the social context (for example, other people) in his therapy. Furthermore, Erickson placed great emphasis on engaging a patient's motivation and attention, thus establishing the "therapist plus client" system as a major context for change. Thus, while his problem focus may have emphasized the individual, his solution focus clearly seemed to be the individual-in-relationship. This is neither a purely monadic viewpoint nor a purely systems viewpoint, but something different altogether.

The weakest part of Fisch's position is his dismissal of hypnosis and the idea of the unconscious as irrelevant, or perhaps obstructive, to further development of Erickson's contributions. Fisch indicates his discomfort with these central aspects of Erickson's work in discrediting them as "mysterious" and overly elaborate. His implication that attention to Erickson's hypnotic techniques has caused inattention to Erickson's ideas of depathologizing problems and interpersonal influence is spurious at best. His contention that "reification of 'the unconscious' will limit the expansions of Erickson's seminal contributions" is indisputable but misleading: Reification of *any* metaphor, whether it be "the unconscious," "the system," or "God," will hinder progress. Thus, the more relevant question is: How can we avoid reification in our thinking?

Finally, Fisch's suggestion that using hypnotic approaches will tend to make therapy longer is unfounded and unwarranted. If anything, it could be argued that hypnosis, especially when applied within a context emphasizing systemic and depathologized views, enables briefer therapy. This seemed to be the case in Erickson's work, and it certainly is so in my own practice.

Taken together, Fisch's comments about hypnosis and "the unconscious" seem to reflect a position that rejects all that is poetic, mythical, experiential, or metaphorical. My own view is that better therapy results may be achieved via a balance of prose and poetry, behavior and experience, rational and hypnotic process. Erickson demonstrated that, in contrast to the tradition of psychoanalysis, this can be done in a pragmatic and grounded fashion. Using hypnosis and the metaphor of the unconscious needn't obscure and confuse; it can, when used properly, enable more creative and effective therapies. I hope Erickson's examples in this regard are extended rather than dismissed or trivialized.

All this is not to say that anyone interested in building on Erickson's work must use hypnosis. Clearly, therapists should employ those techniques and ideas that work for them in producing demonstrable results. Hypnosis works for me, but apparently not for Richard Fisch. Such differences are to be expected and encouraged. Still, I would suggest that rejecting the experiential/metaphorical expressions embodied by hypnotic processes will hinder, not help, progress in the field of therapy.

Milton Erickson's Lesson

Bradford P. Keeney, Ph.D., and Douglas G. Flemons, Ph.D.

In the first sentence of his position paper, Richard Fisch promises to "promote dialogue" and "not impart new information." He has succeeded on both accounts. He brings forth a voice of argument that emphasizes Erickson's contribution to understanding therapy as an arena for solving practical problems in a social context. Although this position was most clearly articulated many years ago by Jay Haley, it is still a fascinating way to begin a conversation. Drawing a distinction and firmly championing one side is always an enticement to lively discussion.

We have little interest in whether Erickson contributed a new paradigm, a new school, a new technique, or a new idea. We believe, however, that he left a lesson for future therapeutic generations. Namely, the key to effective clinical work is to utilize whatever resources may advance the client's situation.

Milton Erickson would play with whatever metaphor, layer of meaning, or technique circumstances evoked. He did short-term *and* long-term therapy; he depathologized *and* he pathologized behaviors; he could be simple and straightforward *and* complex and obscure; he would demystify *and* mystify; he operated as a change agent *and* a stability agent; he was direct *and* indirect; he used language sensitively *and* he used it like a sledgehammer; he didn't rely on medical interventions *and* he is known to have prescribed electroshock; he worked monadically *and* interpersonally; he spoke to the conscious *and* to the unconscious.

A pervasive reading of Erickson's clinical accounts makes it impossible to conveniently categorize which metaphors best characterize his understanding or practice of therapy. Rather than argue about what he *really*

Address correspondence to: Bradford P. Keeney, Ph.D., Counseling Psychology, College of St. Thomas, P.O. Box 5017, 2115 Summit Avenue, St. Paul, MN 55105, or Douglas G. Flemons, Ph.D., 4711 N. W. 24th Circle, #207, Lauderdale Lakes, FL 33313.

thought or did (or should have thought or done), we pose the question derived from Erickson's lesson: How can his work, or anyone's work, be utilized?

Fisch's paper directs us to reexamine and challenge the metaphors of the unconscious (translate "monadic") and to expand Erickson's contributions into the metaphors of the interpersonal (translate "MRI"). We prefer to avoid addiction to either class of metaphor; working exclusively within any domain limits possibilities. Are there clinical cases where therapists suffer from an impasse due to being stuck in a particular metaphor? Let us pretend that the following two syndromes could be found:

1) Therapists at war with the "unconscious." Fits are sometimes triggered by the mere mention of the word. These individuals pepper all social interactions with the phrase "social context" and can often be heard muttering, "Who-did-what-to-whom-when?"

2) Therapists with an unconscious compulsion for uttering the term "unconscious." The afflicted unconsciously embed the word in all written and oral discourse. Hardly a sentence goes by without some unconscious reference to their own or someone else's unconscious. This behavior tends to grate unconsciously on family, friends, and associates.

How could these syndromes be therapeutically encountered? Treatment plans could be organized to demonstrate to the former clinical population the disadvantages of using social process metaphors in a monadic way and the advantages of using unconscious metaphors as a social tactic. Similarly, the latter group could be challenged to consider how social process metaphors provide a way of relating to a client who unconsciously resists conscious talk about unconscious metaphors.

Erickson's lesson simply orients therapists to utilize what clients present. If unconscious metaphors are conveyed, the interactional therapist has a semantic bridge for mediating social change. Similarly, interpersonal metaphors and understandings provide psychodynamic therapists with political bridges to addressing the organization of mind. Given this orientation, it should be clear that we would never critique the Fisch paper along any of the following lines:

1) "Change" is simply a metaphor. Addiction to a metaphor—be it "change," "power," or whatever—can produce unpleasant side effects such as impasses in therapeutic understanding.

2) "Depathologizing" maintains the notion of "pathologizing" because one requires the latter in order to understand the former. This is a solution that maintains the problem.

3) The distinction between concept and technique (or, theory and practice) is less interesting than how therapists conceptualize practice and practice their concepts.

4) Do we really want Erickson's work *not* "to mean all things to all people"? Is it not useful to adapt our explanations of therapy to mesh with the conceptual net of our audiences?

Again, we want to emphasize that we believe the above points are arguments largely disconnected from Erickson's lesson. With this understanding, we are most grateful to Richard Fisch for his paradoxical interventions into the metaphors of therapists interested in Milton Erickson's work. He has expertly demonstrated that it is less elegant to tell clients directly what they need to do and say. Rather, in Ericksonian fashion, he has created a climate that indirectly encourages clients (in this case colleagues in the psychotherapy community) to rebel and come up with their own ideas that are most appropriate for their particular needs.

More Than a Doorway,
A Shift in Epistemology

William J. Matthews, Ph.D.

In November of 1987, one of my doctoral students showed me the *Sunday Parade* section of the local newspaper. Following the always informative questions and answers about celebrities was a featured article about a "new" therapy in which the therapist got his patient to act in unusual ways. Patients were told such things as to stay awake during periods of insomnia; parents were told to teach their obstreperous child how to throw a "proper" tantrum. Already depressed clients were told to plan to be depressed during a certain time of the day. The implication of the article was that one can get clients to do what the therapist wants (namely, that which is ultimately the best for the client) by simply telling them to do the opposite. Of course Milton H. Erickson, M.D., was mentioned as the main founder of such "reverse psychology" techniques. Many of us who consider ourselves to be "Ericksonian" have come to know such interventions as paradoxical injunctions, symptom prescriptions, rituals, etc. and understand these interventions to be the essence of Milton Erickson.

I am in agreement with Dr. Fisch that these interventions are not the main contribution of Erickson. An exclusive emphasis on Erickson's techniques misses the mark. The newspaper story stimulated my worst fear—that Erickson's work will be reduced to a set of popularized techniques that therapists think they can add to their repertoire without regard to the epistemological assumptions that underlie all therapists' behavior. Fisch contends that Erickson created at least two "doorways" through which we can walk: 1) the depathologizing of human behavior; and 2) the use of language as the tool of influence. I agree that Erickson's

The author would like to acknowledge Lynn Hoffman, A.C.S.W., for her helpful comments in the preparation of this rejoinder. Address correspondence to: William J. Matthews, Ph.D., 8 Dwight Circle, Amherst, MA 01002 techniques created a range of possible pathways through these important doorways.

My position is that Fisch has not gone far enough in speaking of the broader implications of Erickson's work because he fails to mention the underlying shift in perceiving the world that these ideas contain. The challenge to the traditional notion of pathology and the use of language for the creation of new meaning are more than content-level reframes. They are the basis for an important epistemological shift from an *objective reality* to a *constructed reality*. This shift in epistemology is the heart of the matter.

This shift in thinking with respect to human systems began with the Bateson research project in Palo Alto in 1952, with Jay Haley, Don Jackson, John Weakland, William Fry, and of course Gregory Bateson. The implications of general systems theory and cybernetics were considered in relation to human interaction. Of particular interest was the pattern of communication in so-called schizophrenic families. There was a shift from a linear Newtonian anticontextual emphasis on objects to an emphasis on the pattern between objects within an observed context. Schizophrenia was considered as a pattern of communication between individuals rather than as a disease located within an individual. In a cybernetic framework, the object apart from its context has no meaning. During this time period, members of the Bateson project also became interested in the work of this strange psychiatrist in Phoenix. In the late 1950s the project disbanded and the Mental Research Institute was created under the direction of Don Jackson.

While the epistemological considerations of Bateson were important to this newly formed group, the dramatic work of Erickson had a significant influence on its approach to therapy. Bateson believed in the importance of theory and epistemology. Erickson was different. One aspect of the Erickson legacy was the opinion that he had no theory of personality. He did what worked. The implication of Erickson's atheoretical view continues to reverberate in a less useful way for subsequent generations of therapists.

I think the problem has become that many Ericksonians appear to eschew theory. Pragmatics, what works, has become the rule. The subtlety of Bateson's ecosystemic and cybernetic view has been pushed aside for "Ericksonian" pragmatic techniques. This argument of pragmatics versus aesthetics was raised in the March 1982 issue of *Family Process* by Bradford Keeney with Douglas Sprenkle (1982) and by Lawrence Allman (1982). These authors used Batesonian arguments to challenge the narrow focus of the strategic approach as created by the MRI and Haley. As one may remember, these authors were severely criticized for their position.

Hoffman (1986) contends that the vehemence of the criticism had a stifling effect on the debate. The issues raised in that debate were significant and bear reconsideration.

First of all, this notion of depathologizing client behavior has important epistemological assumptions behind it. Pathology is based on the assumption of an objective reality. The observer is just a "fact finder" who merely reports what is there. An individual is observed by the objective professional and determined to have some pathology, such as schizophrenia, paranoia, depression, etc. This position implies that the observer is *independent* of (and hierarchical to) what is observed. Radical constructivists such as Heinz von Foerster (1981), Ernst von Glasersfeld (1984), and of course Gregory Bateson (1972) reject the idea of an objective reality. Their contention is that the observer is *always* a part of that which is observed. We do not discover what is out there (such as with DSM-III categories); rather, we *invent* it. In making an observation, the observer is commenting on him- or herself. For example, medical researchers recently noted the effect of the observer on the "white coat" hypertension syndrome. They observed that the hypertension of some patients (typically young women) increased when the observer was a male doctor. The implications for treatment are significant. Social scientists seem reluctant to appreciate what the physical scientists understand—that the act of observing affects what is observed. How we choose to observe clients, based on how we construe the world, determines what we observe.

Erickson was a constructivist in that he rejected the traditional ideas of pathology and the pejorative stigma attached to such diagnoses. He chose to view a client's problematic behavior as logical and as a potential resource to be developed. It was as if he were a human dialysis machine through which negative attributions were filtered. The case of the woman whom he told to spit a stream of water through the "horrible gap" between her teeth (Haley, 1973) is a good example of constructing a different meaning around a problem. However, in my view, the idea that the therapist is not separate from that which is observed was not evident in Erickson's thinking nor in that of those who followed him. We continue to have a normative (and therefore desired) view of individual and family development (e.g., Haley, 1973). Therapists continue to discover the "objective facts" of the dysfunctional family and to plan interventions to "cure" them.

Harry Goolishian (Anderson et al., 1986) attributes much of this thinking to a Parsonian world view (Parsons, 1950), adopted by many family therapists, in which each system is constrained by the next higher system. The individual is constrained by the family which is constrained by the community, etc. Anderson et al. noted that this view carries the idea of "hierarchy of control and power directed from above and harnessed by social role" (p. 1). Thus, the family "causes" a dysfunction in the individual, the community in the family, and so on. The therapist who is an "objective observer" and, by implication, hierarchical to this client system can bring about a cure by correcting the observed dysfunction. This is the same old linear trap of objective reality and causality. Therapists armed with "correct" ideas of the developmentally appropriate family/client apply various techniques to "cause" the desired change. Such therapist behavior can often lead to an exacerbation of the client symptom and therapist angst over not curing the client.

Fisch's second observation that Erickson studied communication for the purpose of influence and change is problematic for me if the implication is that such communication is unidirectional—only from Erickson to the client rather than a recursive loop between Erickson and the client (Matthews, 1985). The problem in a unidirectional view of communication is a linear notion of putting the "right" information into the client to cause change. Thus, it appears to me that many Ericksonian therapists, in adopting a linear view, attempt to find the "correct" story, prescription, ritual, etc. to give to the client to cause the desired change. Such a position contains serious problems and misses the point of a constructed reality rather than an objective reality.

Humberto Maturana, the Chilean biologist and a leading thinker of the new epistemology, takes the position that we are "informationally closed systems" and that information cannot be put in a person like a deposit in a bank (Maturana & Varela, 1987). How we respond to external stimuli is analogous to music and the compact disk (L. Hoffman, personal communication, June 1987). The computer does not have a direct correspondence to the music outside of it. There are no little musicians on the CD. The computer makes its own meaning of the musical stimuli based on its internal structure. Thus, it perceives the music as a series of binary bits of information and encodes these values on the disk. When the disk is played for the listener, based on the listener's structure, it is perceived as music. Analogously, the therapist does not put information *into* the client but rather the client makes meaning of the therapist's words based on his or her internal structures. This is the essence of the use of metaphor. Each client makes his or her own meaning out of the story told. The construction of the metaphor is the result of the interaction between the client and therapist, not a story that is imposed on the client by the correct thinking therapist.

The importance of language cannot be overemphasized. Language is not a simple descriptive mapping of reality but a dialogic process (implying a communication with at least one other) of creating reality. Our language constructs what we observe; for instance, belief in dysfunctional structures creates our observation of such structures in a self-reinforcing loop.

Clients' problems also occur in language. A problem is that which is communicated to another as a problem. Anderson et al. (1986) suggest that it is the problem that determines the system, not the reverse. Systems, such as families, do not "cause" problems, instead, the problem defines the system, namely, those who linguistically share the problem. The idea of family, couples, and/or individual therapy thus may not be relevant, since the treatment unit is defined as all those who share the problem. Importantly, this view allows the therapist to move away from the notion of dysfunctional systems causing the problem, and with it imposing a cure based on some idea of objective reality of the way a system/structure ought to function. Change occurs in how the individual describes him- or herself in relation to others who are connected to the problem discussed. When the problem is no longer defined as a problem, it ceases to exist.

In discussing a constructivist view of therapy, Hoffman (1986) emphasizes six characteristics which distinguish it from a strategic approach. They are: 1) the therapist as part of that which is observed; 2) a collaborative view of reality rather than one that is hierarchically imposed; 3) goals that emphasize setting the context for new meaning to occur rather than specifying the correct new meaning; 4) ways to guard against too much instrumentality; 5) a multiverse view—many explanations each with legitimacy; 6) a nonpejorative view of the client—all problems have a logic and fit.

Erickson was a pioneer and innovator who challenged ideas that were constraining to him. What his epistemological assumptions were we cannot know. We cannot, however, arbitrarily apply his techniques without considering our own epistemological assumptions about the world. To use technique to "cause the desired change that we know would be best" for our clients is to support an expert/dummy, hierarchical model of therapy, which seems antithetical to the Ericksonian view that clients make the best choices for themselves at any given moment. The result of such action can be a symmetrical escalation between client and therapist, often with negative attributions ascribed to the intransigent client.

A constructivist, nonobjective view of the world suggests that therapy is a conversation that can have the potential for the construction of new meaning for all the participants. The therapist moves from the restrictive role of expert to that of collaborator in the construction of new meaning, a different reality. In this view, loading up with technique to hunt down defective prey does not lead to useful clinical work. For me, the "doorways" created by Erickson of which Fisch speaks are better seen as "portals" to a different dimension of knowing the world. In that world, Erickson's techniques are much less important than the meaning that underlies them.

References

Allman, L. (1982). The aesthetic preference. *Family Process, 21*, 43–56.

Anderson, H., Goolishian, H., & Winderman, L. (1986). Problem determined systems: Towards transformation in family therapy. *Journal of Strategic and Systemic Therapies, 5*(4), 1–14.

Bateson, G. (1972). Steps to an ecology of mind. New York: Ballantine.

Haley, J. (1973). *Uncommon therapy.* New York: Norton.

Hoffman, L. (1986). Beyond power and control: Toward a second order family systems therapy. *Family Systems Medicine, 3*, 381–396.

Keeney, B., & Sprenkle, D. (1982). Ecosystemic epistemology. *Family Process, 21*, 1–21.

Maturana, H. & Varela, F. (1987). *The tree of knowledge: The biological roots of human understanding.* Boston: New Science Library.

Matthews, W. (1985). A cybernetic model of psychotherapy: One hand draws the other. *Elements and dimensions of an Ericksonian approach* (Ericksonian Monographs, *1*, pp. 42–60). New York: Brunner/Mazel.

Parsons, T. (1950). The prospects of sociological theory. *American Sociological Review, 15*, 3–16.

von Foerster, H. (1981). *Observing systems.* Seaside, CA: Intersystems.

von Glaserfeld, E. (1984). An introduction to radical constructivism. In P. Watzlawick (Ed.), *The invented reality.* New York: Norton.

Conflict Between Development of a New Research Tradition and of Social Technology: A Conceptual Problem

William R. Nugent, Ph.D.

Dr. Fisch expresses concern in his position paper that professionals, in using Erickson's reported ideas and methods, will:

> fail to build on the *conceptual* doorways implicit in his work and instead focus on emulations or elaborations of what might be called his technique. As a result, opportunities will be missed for the development of new ideas and approaches for solving personal, interpersonal, and social problems.

He further expresses his view that the major potential impact of Erickson's work lies in two conceptual "bridges to the development of more effective ways of resolving human problems," the

> *context* or concept of "trance" [which] allowed him to develop a discipline of human influence, and the *metaphor* of "unconscious as benign" [which] gave him the freedom to depathologize human problems.

Fisch concludes that a focus on the replication of Erickson's clinical methods will obscure these conceptual bridges and that "emphasis on such things as hypnotic techniques and 'addressing the patient's unconscious' will tend to make treatments longer, not shorter."

Let me, like Fisch, state my position at the beginning:

Address correspondence to: William R. Nugent, Ph.D., 3238 Citation Trail, Tallahassee, FL 32308

1) Erickson's methods and ideas are congruent with current development of the behavioral research tradition and no compelling need for a new tradition has yet been demonstrated; and

2) Erickson's techniques must be replicated and developed further as crucial first steps in the development of a new theoretical or research tradition, should one be developed.

First let me elaborate my position in a less technical manner. After this general discussion, I will provide a somewhat more technical framework for viewing Fisch's concerns, drawing from recent ideas in the philosophy of science.

General Response

Fisch's concerns may be seen as a conflict between development of "Ericksonian" techniques under some existent or nonexistent theoretical tradition and the development of "Ericksonian" techniques under a yet to be developed, new "Ericksonian" theoretical tradition (by "theoretical tradition" is meant a broad, general conceptual system which serves as a base for development of more specific models and technology). Fisch is concerned that professionals using Erickson's ideas and methods will focus upon the replication, development, and elaboration of clinical procedures, that is, upon the *elaboration and development of a series of specific intervention models, or intervention technology* (such as hypnotic techniques). Further, he is concerned that *these specific theories will be developed at the expense of a broader development of a new theoretical tradition, an "Ericksonian" tradition.* This latter development would involve, presumably, the elaboration of such concepts as "trance" and "the benign unconscious." Fisch expresses concern that a focus on development of intervention theory, or social technology, would obscure important conceptual bridges (trance and benign unconscious), inhibit both the development of an "Ericksonian" theoretical tradition and the integration of Ericksonian concepts into general systems theory, and would "tend to make treatments longer, not shorter."

In a strict and limited sense, Fisch is correct: A predominant focus on techniques for providing adequate solutions to treatment problems faced by clinicians would, almost by definition, slow the development of a broad Ericksonian conceptual system (an Ericksonian theoretical tradition). If few focus upon the development of a truly new general conceptual system for viewing human problems, development of such a broad theory will be slow and, in a sense, out of the mainstream.

In a broader sense, one must ask a couple of crucial questions before deciding the importance of this conceptual problem. First, is a new theoretical tradition *needed*? Fisch emphasizes several times Erickson's "nonpathologized" approach to human problems. The behavioral tradition *also* takes this approach to human problems (Bandura, 1969, pp. 1–19; Nay, 1976, pp. 1–12; Rimm & Masters, 1979, pp. 4–12). While earlier versions of the behavioral theoretical tradition eschewed use of "inferred states" or "private events" (such as thoughts and feelings) in behavioral theories and techniques, more recent evolution in this tradition has brought not only thoughts and feelings into behavioral models but also concepts such as a "creative unconscious" (Beck, 1976; Burns, 1980; Meichenbaum, 1984).

Hypnosis and "trance" have also been used in the behavioral tradition, as has Erickson's tailor-fitting treatment to the individual client (Lazarus, 1976; Rimm & Masters, 1979, pp. 4–12). Thus, it would seem that a new theoretical tradition is *not* necessary in order to extend and develop Erickson's ideas and concepts. The behavioral tradition, in its current evolution, seems well suited as a conceptual umbrella for Ericksonian hypnosis and therapy, especially in light of this tradition's emphasis on the *interaction between individual and environment* (Johnston & Pennypacker, 1980).

Development of Ericksonian concepts and technology within the behavioral research tradition would have the added advantage of belonging within a tradition that *demands* the empirical validation of intervention technology. This would help prevent Ericksonian methods from being used in orthodox, "Canon Law" fashion, as many methods have been used (Tennov, 1976). It would also prohibit reliance on an a priori assumption from a theoretical tradition that the tradition's clinical methods are effective, only to have the methods later found empirically to be ineffective clinical tools, as other traditions have had happen (Giles, 1983a, 1983b; Tennov, 1976).

A second, important question is: Is it likely that emphasis on the development of specific intervention technology (such as hypnotic techniques) will make treatment last longer rather than shorter? This concern constitutes an *empirical problem,* not a conceptual problem, answerable through empirical methods. Empirical evidence would seem to suggest that the *reverse may be true: Emphasis on the development of effective clinical technology may well function to speed up effective treatment.*

Many writers have described an almost backward approach to solving human problems taken by the helping professions (Fischer, 1978; Tennov, 1976). Elaborate causal/developmental theories about human problems are developed with the implicit assumption that a theory of problem development necessarily provides ways and means of *changing* problems.Such a course has been taken, for example, by the psychoanalytic tradition, with the result that their clinical methods continually fail to be demonstrated as effective social technology (Giles, 1983a, 1983b; Tennov, 1976).

In comparison, the behavioral tradition evolved out of experimental development of techniques for controlling and changing behavior, as opposed to arising from nonexperimentally based theoretical formulations (Johnston & Pennypacker, 1980; Rimm & Masters, 1979). Empirical evidence suggests that behavioral methods are not only superior to those of other traditions but also more economical in terms of time (Giles, 1983a, 1983b; Rimm & Masters, 1979). Thus, the behavioral research tradition, at this time, apparently has been able to provide more adequate solutions to empirical problems of concern to clinical practitioners than have other traditions (such as the psychoanalytic). This suggests that the behavioral tradition is, at this time, more progressive than other traditions, namely more effective at providing effective and economical clinical intervention techniques.[1]

Further, Erickson himself was atheoretical and, apparently, developed effective technology sans the holding of strong theoretical beliefs (Haley, 1973, Lankton & Lankton, 1983). Indeed, if one reads his collected works and follows the evolution of Erickson's ideas and technique, it can be seen that he essentially developed methods through clinical experiment and, only incidentally, began to develop concepts explaining what he did. This might explain his comments that other writers could explain better than he what he did (see, for example, Bandler & Grinder, 1975).[2] Thus, Erickson demonstrated that a broad theoretical tradition is not a necessary prerequisite to effective social technology—and effective social technology is the life blood of the helping professions (Fischer, 1978; Thomas, 1978).

Current Philosophy of Science

These concerns can profitably be viewed from a perspective elaborated by Larry Laudan (1977) in his writing on scientific progress. Laudan defines two broad types of "problems" that have occupied investigators in all fields: *empirical problems* and *conceptual problems*. An empirical problem is a substantive question about the entities or objects in some domain of interest. For example, empirical problems that might concern a number of social disciplines are: "What makes some individuals physically abuse children?" and "What clinical procedure used with client B, who faints anytime her skin is pierced by a hypodermic needle, will result in her remaining awake and alert any time her skin is pierced by a hypodermic needle?" (Nugent, 1987).

Empirical problems are the *fundamental questions* for which a discipline must provide "adequate answers." In the helping professions the empirical questions concern, among other things, the ways and means for reliably inducing change in some defined condition. Such a set of ways and means may be seen to constitute a social technology (or set of techniques), what Fischer (1978) refers to as "intervention theories," *without which a helping profession cannot exist* (Thomas, 1978). In the case of social technology, "adequate answers" to empirical problems can be defined as clinical procedures—techniques—that *reliably work;* procedures that, when used, at a bare minimum, reliably (replication after replication) increase the probability that client B will change from defined state X_1 to defined state X_2. Ideally, the probability of change from state X_1 to state X_2 when the treatment is used with client B will approach 1.0, a probability that indicates a social technology—a technique—of high dependability and utility.

A *conceptual problem*, on the other hand, is a question about conceptual systems (or, synonymously in this paper, theories) created to answer empirical problems. A conceptual problem is peculiar to a particular theory, is literally created by the existence of the theory, and has no existence without existence of the theory. Conceptual problems concern both the internal structure of a theory and how a particular theory fits with other "accepted" conceptual systems. For example, the conflict between Biblical accounts of the creation of mankind and Darwinian theories of evolution is an exemplar of an external conceptual problem.[3] The types of theories with which a particular conceptual system can conflict, and thereby create a conceptual problem for b*o*th theories, can be informal "social beliefs," religious or ethical systems, scientific theories, methodological systems, and broad conceptual systems about the nature of the world.

Laudan (1977) describes two general classes of theories: theories specific to particular phenomena and that can be used to generate specific predictions (such as "procedure Y will cause person B to change from state X_1 to state X_2) and broad, very general conceptual systems which: 1) describe general presuppositions about the world; 2) define the general types of concepts allowed in specific theories; and 3) describe the preferred ways and means of answering questions about specific phenomena of interest. This latter type of theory is called by Laudan a "research tradition," a concept very similar to Kuhn's "paradigm" (Kuhn, 1970), or Lakatos's "research programme" (Laudan, 1977), and cannot be used to generate specific predictions about phenomena.

Phenomena-specific theories, which address specific empirical problems, are created, according to Laudan (1977), under the auspices of a particular research tradition. The research tradition provides a *presupposi-*

tional base for these specific theories, mandates the type of concepts that may and may not be used in specific theories, and mandates how new knowledge is to be generated and evaluated. For example, early in its development the behavioral research tradition allowed only concepts tied to publicly observable phenomena to be used in theories and mandated that all specific theories must be empirically validated (Johnston & Pennypacker, 1980). However, as Laudan (1977) describes, research traditions evolve and change over time. Recent evolution in the behavioral research tradition allows use of publicly nonobservable phenomena (such as thoughts and feelings) in theoretical formulations, while the requirement of empirical validation remains a mainstay of the tradition (Phillips, 1981; Rimm & Masters, 1979). Thus, Fisch's concerns may be seen as defining an external conceptual problem: developing Erickson's techniques and conceptualizations under an existing research tradition (or sans the presuppositional base of an existing research tradition) versus developing a new presuppositional base, namely, a new research tradition, prior to any extensive focus upon replication and further development of Erickson's intervention techniques. Erickson's methods and conceptualizations, apparently in Fisch's view, are incompatible with existing research traditions, and with implicit methodological views that a research tradition *must* exist prior to development and replication of effective clinical technology.

Summary

In a strict sense, Fisch is correct: Emphasis upon replication and further development of Erickson's intervention technology will, almost by definition, inhibit mainstream development of a new research, or theoretical, tradition. *But is this an undesirable state of affairs?* There seem to be compelling reasons why the answer to this is a strong *"No—it is NOT an undesirable state of affairs."* The helping professions have repeatedly demonstrated that a well-articulated research tradition does not necessarily provide effective social technology (Tennov, 1976). However, a focus upon development of effective behavior change techniques *prior to explication of a new research tradition* has brought about not only effective social technology, but also an evolving and progressive new research tradition—the behavioral tradition—with which Erickson's methods and conceptualizations are quite compatible (Johnston & Pennypacker, 1980).

This all suggests that it may well be a mistake to put development of a fully articulated research tradition before replication and development of Erickson's clinical tools. Indeed, it may well be a strong argument *for developing reliable social technology first and using the reliable, effective techniques as first steps in development of a new research tradition,* if it is deemed necessary to develop a new tradition. If this is so, the replication of *both* Erickson's methods and results are crucially more important at this point than articulating new concepts. This is particularly true since there is some question as to whether Erickson achieved his results through replicable procedures or by virtue of his powerful personal force (or, perhaps, a combination of both) (Simon, 1983). In this way it can be demonstrated that Erickson left us much more than just the legend of a man whose unique personal power enabled him to evoke dramatic and often rapid change in human problems.

Notes

1. This should not be taken as implying behavioral theories provide "truth" in some Platonic sense. It *does* demonstrate, however, that the behavioral tradition has been more successful than others in providing effective and reliable social technology. Following Laudan's (1977) discussion of the adequacy of a research tradition, this success of the behavioral tradition over time in providing more adequate social technology than "rival" research traditions is a strong point in favor of developing Ericksonian methods under its conceptual umbrella.
2. This is a most interesting comment for a brilliant therapist to make. It leads directly to the question of how accurate the "describers" are in describing and explaining his work. The construct validity of the conceptualizations of Erickson's clinical procedures (empirical operations) created by these "describers" is *not* granted a priori, regardless of how elegant and appealing they may be conceptually.
3. For some religious systems there is not a conceptual conflict between religious tenets and Darwinian evolutionary theories. One example is Mormonism. This religious system "allows" Darwinian conceptualizations to be compatible with its tenets by conceptualizing, for example, that seven of God's days are different from seven of man's; that evolution could well be a means used by God for creating mankind.

References

Bandler, R., & Grinder, J. (1975). *Patterns of the hypnotic techniques of Milton H. Erickson* (Vol. 1). Cupertino, CA: Meta.

Bandura, A. (1969). *Principles of behavior modification.* New York: Holt, Rinehart, & Winston.

Beck, A. (1976). *Cognitive therapy and the emotional disorders.* New York: New American Library.

Burns, D. (1980). *Feeling good: The new mood therapy.* New York: New American Library.

Fischer, J. (1978). *Effective casework practice.* New York: McGraw-Hill.

Giles, T. (1983a). Probable superiority of behavioral interventions: traditional comparative outcomes. *Journal of Behavior Therapy & Experimental Psychiatry, 14,* 29–32.

Giles, T. (1983b). Probable superiority of behavioral interventions: empirical status of the equivalence of therapies hypothesis. *Journal of Behavior Therapy & Experimental Psychiatry, 14,* 189–196.

Haley, J. (1973). *Uncommon therapy.* New York: Norton.

Johnston, J., & Pennypacker, H. (1980). *Strategies and tactics of human behavioral research.* Hillsdale, NJ: Lawrence Erlbaum.

Kuhn, T. (1970). *The structure of scientific revolutions.* Chicago: University of Chicago Press.

Lankton, S., & Lankton, C. (1983). *The answer within.* New York: Brunner/Mazel.

Laudan, L. (1977). *Progress and its problems.* Berkeley, CA: University of California Press.

Lazarus, A. (1976). *Multimodal behavior therapy.* New York: Springer.

Meichenbaum, D. (1984). Workshop presented in Jacksonville, Florida.

Nay, W. (1976). *Behavioral intervention.* New York: Gardner.

Nugent, W. (1987). The use and evaluation of theories. *Social Work Research and Abstracts,* Winter, 14–19.

Phillips, L. (1981). Roots and branches of behavioral and cognitive practice. *Journal of Behavior Therapy & Experimental Psychiatry, 12,* 5–17.

Rimm, D., & Masters, J. (1979). *Behavior therapy* (2nd ed.). Orlando, FL: Academic.

Simon, R. (1983). Erickson's way. *The Family Therapy Networker, 7,* 21–27.

Tennov, D. (1976). *Psychotherapy: The hazardous cure.* New York: Anchor.

Thomas, E. J. (1978). Generating innovation in social work: the paradigm of developmental research. *Journal of Social Service Research, 2,* 95–115.

The Art of the Possible

Robert E. Pearson, M.D.

As I read Dr. Fisch's article for the first time I was bemused to remember something that happened about 30 years ago. A young physician had just finished presenting his first paper since medical school to a large audience at an annual meeting of The American Society of Clinical Hypnosis. Milton Erickson asked permission to comment on the presentation and, of course, was welcomed to do so. Impaling the physician with his eyes (Jay Haley's term), Erickson spoke carefully and slowly. "I asked to speak . . . for reasons . . . which are very important . . . to me. . . . I want to say . . . [by now the speaker was experiencing death number 126 of his allotted 1,000] . . . that I quite violently . . . [number 400 flashed by] . . . agree with the ideas and conclusions of the author." As do I with the ideas and conclusions of Dr. Fisch.

I do mildly disagree with Fisch's first statement: "The purpose of a position paper is . . . not to impart new information." When an argument is well thought-out, and then presented with the clarity and elegance demonstrated here, it *does* make a real contribution to knowledge.

Fisch's central theme is that many who call themselves Ericksonian therapists seem to be blinded by the brilliance of Erickson's techniques and, in the "emulation or elaborations" of these, lose sight of his more important contribution, the concept that the symptoms of "mental illness" are the result of *normal* striving for independence, pleasure, or meaning. Some of us have issued similar caveats before, but none so well or succinctly as has Fisch. Personal experience (read "bias") tells me that not all "mental" symptoms in all people are the result of such strivings, that some of them do in fact have diseases of physiology or anatomy. Some people are not "wired" correctly, and some of their problems are the result of that. I am saddened to know that there are some among us who would

Address correspondence to: Robert E. Pearson, M.D., 7887 San Felipe, #248, Houston, TX 77063.

think of that idea as not bias, but rather blasphemy. Thank God that Erickson would not be one of them.

Fisch sees more difference between his view of Erickson's concept of trance and Haley's view than I do. Erickson did not and would not now have trouble with Haley's description of the interaction between hypnotist and patient. Of course the belief of an Erickson, a Haley, or another hundred masters does not make something "true." There may be no strict truths in these matters, but still, our striving to find them are of utmost importance in our struggles to become better change agents. We also must not repeat some parallel to the Sister Kenny debacle, in which physicians were ostracized for using a treatment that *was* useful but "could not work" because the good sister's theory behind it was "obviously nonsense." The success of a treatment does not prove the validity of the theory on which it was built, but the history of medicine and psychotherapy contains hundreds of examples of that backward thinking. Some not so very long ago.

As Fisch points out, Erickson did, for the most part, ask patients to *do* things. But not always. Sometimes he "just told stories." Very carefully thought-out tales, tailored to the patient's needs as specifically as any medical prescription, not just anything that seemed to come to mind that day. Sometimes, in the telling of the same basic story, there would be variations in details and emphasis in order to best suit the needs of that patient. I believe that only rarely did two patients hear exactly the same story; I know I didn't.

When he did ask patients to do things, it was always something he knew they could do, even if the patients were doubtful of their ability to do it. Sometimes he asked them to be sure not to get rid of the symptom yet (!) or even to make the symptom worse. Who but a Milton Erickson would think of doing that as part of therapy? He knew that people are tough.

I have come to think of hypnosis as the art of the possible.

It is really no wonder that so many of us became beguiled by Erickson's mastery of communication. On one occasion I heard him request that a colleague *not* respond to a series of questions he was about to ask. Erickson then asked the questions, and confidently went on to use the "answers" as a basis for further discussion. The colleague was at least as astonished as the rest of us in the group and confirmed that Erickson's "suppositions" were correct. Another time Erickson told some of us how he was able to predict where several people would sit at a table in a room none of them had ever been in. As is most often the case, it was all very mysterious until it was explained: then it was "obvious."

Part of what Fisch calls "an attraction to the elaborate and mysterious" can be laid at Erickson's door. At times, at least while teaching, he did appear to enjoy being "cute." His famous Saturday afternoon demonstrations during the Seminars on Hypnosis and ASCH-ERF workshops of the 1950s and 1960s were frequently so complex that they seemed to be magic shows, demonstrating skills obviously beyond anything that could be learned by ordinary humans. Often we were so taken by the masterful demonstrations that we didn't even ask questions, either because none of us wanted to appear to be stupid, or more likely, because we hadn't received enough information on which to base intelligent inquiries.

Looking back, in some ways the demonstrations were even more marvelous than they appeared to be at the time, but it seems to me that some of the audience mistook their own confusion for an understanding of what they were seeing, and decided that being obscure and/or elaborate was the key to being an Ericksonian therapist.

Sometimes, when asked later, in private, to explain something further, Erickson seemed to be unaware that he had not already clarified the point adequately. Obfuscation or elaboration for its own sake is fumbling, not likely to help many people. Before consulting us, patients have already fumbled, usually a number of times, in their attempts to change—that's why they come to us. Was it his fault or ours that Erickson was not always clear the first (or second, or third) time through? It is a moot point. Those of us who did ask questions should not have waited until only a small group heard his answers. And we could have told him more forcefully that much of what he said that was apparently evident to him was far from being understood by us.

One more item of personal bias. I do wish that we could get rid of the term "hypnotherapy." The word is misleading in that it seems to imply that the hypnosis *is* the therapy, as in chemotherapy and radiotherapy. "We" know what the word really means, but a lot of therapists function as if hypnosis is the cause of change rather than a vehicle for therapy. This point is relevant to a position on Erickson's approach and needs to be expressed.

In summary, Fisch is correct in his ideas and in his conclusions; his concerns are amply justified. We have grieved our loss for nearly 4,000 days, and in some aspects ground has been lost. It's time we got on with the real work at hand.

Understanding Erickson from His Own Point of View

Ernest L. Rossi, Ph.D.

While I am in deep sympathy with Dr. Fisch's effort to depathologize problems and explore the important role of interpersonal influence in psychotherapy, I believe he is misguided in attempting to challenge Erickson's 1) monadic (intrapersonal) approach, 2) Erickson's utilization of the "unconscious" as an important concept in dealing with psychopathology, and 3) Erickson's major contributions to hypnosis.

As Fisch openly acknowledges: "Erickson was monadically oriented." I do not know, however, why Fisch goes on to say, "This must sound strange to many readers." It cannot sound strange to anyone who has actually read Erickson's (1980) *Collected Papers*. Erickson usually worked one-on-one with his patients. Even when two or more family members were present, his typical approach was to use the other family members only as a backdrop for facilitating important intrapersonal therapeutic responses (e.g., Rossi & Ryan, 1985, pp. 27–31). Even the most cursory examination of the papers Erickson wrote himself reveals an intense preoccupation with internal psychodynamics taking place within the individual in a monadic manner. In particular, Volumes II and III of his *Collected Papers* contain the most carefully detailed demonstrations of mental mechanisms and psychopathology that have ever been published in the hypnotic literature.

From whence, then, cometh all the recent rejection of Erickson's major *hypnotic* investigations of the *intrapersonal, unconscious* mechanisms of *psychopathology*? A clue is provided by Hammond (1987):

Milton Erickson seems to have focused much of his energy on *intra*personal work. Over and over again, Erickson worked with

---

Address correspondence to: Ernest L. Rossi, Ph.D., 23708 Harbor Vista, Malibu, CA 90265.

trance phenomenon and suggestion to alter perceptions and mental sets. In contrast, Jay Haley, the Mental Research Institute group, and others have stressed the *inter*personal and paradoxical focus of Erickson's approach. These were part of the breadth of Erickson's creativity and eclectic approach, but are they being overemphasized as the core of his work? I will leave this to the reader to consider as you study Erickson, in his own words. (p. 153)

Many of us are beginning to wonder if MRI is the Grinch Who Stole Erickson! Indeed, examples of an apparently overweening attitude on the part of some MRI people to do away with Erickson's *intra*personal approach and his use of the concept of the unconscious were evident very early in Haley's *Conversations with Milton H. Erickson* (1985). Let us look at some passages from Volume I of that series:

H: . . . You often speak of a patient discovering something when it seems to be a kind of unconscious discovery.

E: Yes.

H: Your structure of the mind sometimes confuses me a bit. The conscious and the unconscious are complicated enough, but when you have the unconscious discovering something, then it gets a little too complicated for me.

E: I expect you know this. What do you see there?

H: It's a square.

E: Now this is what I mean about the unconscious discovering something. You know everything that's there, and you look upon it as a square with diagonals, verticals and horizontals. Yet you know everything that's there. There's a lot more there than what you see.

H: You mean more in terms of planes and things?

E: More in terms of what you see. Because you see this, don't you? And what is that? That's "B." They're all there. There's an "X" there too. There's even a cube. A square cube. Now you saw every one of those parts but you didn't identify them. There's been nothing added to the picture, and you can recognize every individual part. You have now suddenly discovered the alphabet. And you know all the alphabet. You see what I mean? You've often looked at a thing and taken it that way and then all of a sudden you happen to get a different view of it, and why didn't you know it in the first place? You're amazed.

H: Well, that's a conscious discovery though.

E: Can't the unconscious do exactly the same thing, because it just hasn't gotten around to shifting the parts about? In the reasoning process, the two strings. Students would labor for hours on them. Now they know what a pendulum is. All of a sudden they put it together. Their unconscious has known what a pendulum is. They haven't acquired any *new* information; they've just discovered what they have there. And it comes as a flash of unconscious insight.

H: Well, it may be an unconscious insight, but it comes as a flash of conscious insight.

E: Then it comes as a flash of conscious insight, but it first came as a flash of unconscious insight.

H: In your therapy do you often leave a problem at the level of unconscious insight?

E: Yes. Often. "You probably won't be ready to know this consciously for some time, so keep it out of your conscious mind. Filter it through gradually. Don't blow off, with a sudden discovery that you hate your mother."

H: Do you ever use this with them in a waking state? Such a statement as, "Don't discover this consciously"?

E: Yes. But literally I'm speaking on two levels. "Don't discover this consciously," really means, "Unconscious, keep it to yourself for a while." (pp. 98–99)

A few pages later, this theme is picked up again and leads Erickson to challenge Haley with the question, "Are you going to get rid of the back of the mind?" (Erickson's colloquialism for the unconscious):

H: Talking about metaphors or analogies or stories, you have said you reach the unconscious with them.

E: Yes.

H: Now you chose the word "unconscious" as a description of this process. I wonder if it is really essential, or if you could deal with it in terms of how to get someone to follow a suggestion which they cannot resist because they are not aware of it. They are not aware they are receiving the suggestion. An awareness difference, rather than an unconscious-conscious difference.

E: I'm trying to think of a patient. She told me about her horrible self-consciousness in a bathing suit because it seemed to her that whenever she wore a bathing suit her genitals were too prominent and everybody looked at that area of her body. She didn't like to go swimming for that reason. Another thing she mentioned was the question that had come to her, whether or not at the age of 35 she should relinquish her virginity. She wasn't willing to talk about that, and she only talked about the temptations she had had. But she was utterly, utterly indefinite, and so I steered her away from the subject. I knew that she was self-conscious in a bathing suit, everybody looked at her genitals, and that she had, at the age of 35, wondered about the desirability of keeping her virginity. She was a decidedly attractive woman. Of course, if she wanted to wonder about the desirability of keeping her virginity, and she mentioned the age of 35—well, I drew my own conclusion. So one day I told her, "You know, Eisenhower, and Patton and—who was the other general? Suppose you tell me about the Battle of the Bulge?" And I got the whole story about the time she went to bed with a man and then wondered and wondered and fought the man off on the battle of the bulge.

H: Milton, that's a remarkable metaphor. But suppose the idea of conscious and unconscious had never been proposed. Now, how else would you explain what you did in that example? If there was no such concept as the unconscious.

E: *Are you going to get rid of the back of the mind?*

H: Well, how else would you explain the way you slipped the suggestion in? I mean, suppose we were born in 1840 and observing the same phenomenon, but prior to the idea of the unconscious.

As a creative contributor with an *inter*personal point of view, Haley, of course, is free to explore how he can conceptualize human psychology without using a concept of the unconscious. The above passages clearly indicate, however, that it would be a misreading of Erickson to deny his reliance on the use of the unconscious. I know of no evidence that Erickson thought of the unconscious as a metaphor, as Fisch suggests when he says, "Reification of his use of the 'unconscious' metaphor will, likewise, cloud the fullest implications of a depathologized view about problems." The essence of Erickson's naturalistic or utilization approach was to access and activate the patient's own real unconscious resources to facilitate problem solving and healing.

It is very interesting and important to note that after the above exchange between Haley and Erickson, the topic of the unconscious completely disappears! The word *unconscious* is not even listed in the indexes of Volumes II and III of Haley's *Conversations with Milton H. Erickson.* If we can assume that Haley has published an accurate account, we can only conclude that since Haley did not heed Erickson's mildly challenging query, "Are you going to get rid of the back of the mind?", Erickson decided to drop his own intrapersonal frame of reference and adopt

Haley's interpersonal frame. Erickson adopted the point of view Haley obviously wished to explore. There then followed a generation of creative exchange between Erickson and the MRI group exploring psychopathology on an interpersonal level. As we all know, this illustrates a singular characteristic of Erickson's genius: He would quickly sense and adopt whatever frame of reference his patients or students had and proceed to *utilize* it to heal and teach them within the metaphors of their own mind.

When, exactly 20 years later, in 1972, I began my intensive program of study and writing with Erickson, I was almost completely innocent of the extent of all his previous work with the MRI group. With hindsight, however, I now realize that something very similar happened within the crucial first few sessions of my work with Erickson. At the time (and even now), I had a strongly humanistic and Jungian orientation, and I would blather on and on using words like *psychosynthesis, growth, identity, evolving consciousness,* and the like. Erickson seemed to nod wonderfully agreeable assent to it all, until one day I noticed a subtle, wry smile on his face as he summarized a case with, "Or as you would call it, this was *psychosynthesis, an example of growth.*" He seemed to pronounce *psychosynthesis* slowly with what I experienced as a mildly mocking imitation of my apparent reverence for the word. It immediately flashed across my mind that Erickson was beginning to teach me within my own frames of reference! But *I had come to learn how he achieved his therapeutic effects from his own point of view!*

I was shaken by this experience. It led me to quietly resolve to drop my own vocabulary and make every effort to adopt his. I studied all of his papers very carefully—so carefully that he soon decided that I should edit them. My subsequent collaborative volumes with Erickson (Erickson et al., 1976; Erickson & Rossi, 1979, 1981) then took the form of a dialogue between a seemingly naive student and a mature therapist. This "naive attitude" was criticized by the early readers and reviewers of those volumes. It was the only approach available to me, however, that enabled a presentation of Erickson *within his own frames of reference.* I have no illusions about the extent of my success, but our collaboration was at least an honest effort made with some awareness of the problems involved in the integration of two very different points of view.

During the writing of our first book, *Hypnotic Realities* (Erickson et al., 1976), for example, we agreed that I would use scrupulous care in presenting his own words and concepts verbatim in all of our co-authored publications. Andre Weitzenhoffer, who has long been celebrated for his thorough German scholarship, carefully studied the original manuscript of *Hypnotic Realities* and, together with Erickson and I, spent almost a week going over it practically line by line to make sure it was faithful to the actual words and spirit of Erickson's point of view. When Weitzenhoffer then wrote an introduction to the volume, it was no empty gesture; he was documenting the objectivity of the book as an accurate record of Erickson's work from his own point of view.

Erickson and I later agreed that when I wrote my own papers or spoke of his work to others, I was free to use my own vocabulary and frames of reference as long as I carefully distinguished which was which. In particular, we agreed that where he would use the word *manipulate,* I could use the word *facilitate;* where he used the word *technique,* I could use the word *approach;* where he used *control,* I might use *evoke.* In retrospect, I now see Erickson as a transition figure in the history of hypnosis, particularly in the shift from the older, authoritarian methods and attitudes and the newer permissive approaches he pioneered.

I hope the major difference between the MRI approach to Erickson and my own is now clear. Haley's well-documented work with Erickson illustrates how Erickson adapted himself to facilitating Haley's frame of reference. In my collaborative studies with Erickson, I did the exact reverse by making a definite effort to temporarily adapt myself to Erickson's frame of reference. For Fisch to now write a position paper wherein he denies the essence of Erickson's hypnotic *intra*personal approach to the inner dynamic of unconscious processes in dealing with psychopathology is simply a case of the tail wagging the dog.

With greater justification, I could say that Erickson was basically a "closet Jungian" psychoanalyst because he wrote so many papers about mental mechanisms and even used some of the major concepts that Jung (1979) introduced into the literature, such as "psychological complex" and "inner resynthesis." Certainly, Erickson did use these words himself when he wrote one of his rare definitions of therapy (Erickson, 1948/1980, p. 38):

> The induction and maintenance of a trance serve to provide a *special psychological state in which the patient can reassociate and reorganize his inner psychological complexities* and utilize his own capacities in a manner in accord with his own experiential life. . . . therapy results from an *inner resynthesis* of the patient's behavior achieved by the patient himself. It's true that direct suggestion can effect an alteration in the patient's behavior and result in a symptomatic cure, at least temporarily. However, such a "cure" is simply a response to suggestion and does not entail that reassociation and reorganization of ideas, understandings and memories so essential for actual cure. *It is this experience of reassociating and reorganizing his own experiential life that eventuates in a cure,* not the manifestation of responsive behavior which can, at best, satisfy only the observer.

The case was very different with the term "double bind," which originally came from Gregory Bateson, a guiding light of MRI. Haley shouts with obvious delight, "A use of double binds!" (Erickson et al, 1959/1980, p. 219) when he uncovers them in one of Erickson's transcripts. Erickson had been using double and triple binds long before his interaction with the MRI group. It is a testament to the robust creativity of MRI that Erickson then adopted their term "double bind" in his later discussions of his own work (Erickson & Rossi, 1975/1980). This again illustrates how Erickson adapted to MRI's frames in relation to them rather then vice versa. A more detailed analysis of the contrasting use of the double bind on an interpersonal level by MRI and Erickson's tendency to use it on an intrapersonal level was presented at the 1983 National Meetings of the American Society of Clinical Hypnosis (Rossi & Jichaku, 1983). This material will be published in Rossi and Ryan (1990).

I believe the interpersonal point-of-view has very important contributions to make in a world that is torn with such catastrophic interpersonal tensions as ours is today. But I also believe in the autonomy and independence of the individual working within her/himself on an intrapersonal level as an important aspect of growth and maturity. The interpersonal and intrapersonal points-of-view are complementary; we need both in any well-balanced approach to the theory and practice of psychotherapy.

I very much agree with Fisch when he ends his paper with the words, "My hope, of course, is that we will be free to examine and challenge ideas and techniques, even Erickson's, so that we can build on his daring and important contributions." It is also my hope that we will study carefully what Erickson actually wrote and did without trying to reframe him into something he was not.

References

Erickson, M. (1948/1980). Hypnotic psychotherapy. In E. Rossi (Ed.), *The collected papers of Milton H. Erickson on hypnosis. Vol. IV. Innovative hypnotherapy*. New York: Irvington, pp. 35–48.

Erickson, M. (1980). *The collected papers of Milton H. Erickson on hypnosis* (4 vols). (E. L. Rossi, Ed.). New York: Irvington.

Erickson, M., Haley, J., & Weakland, J. (1959/1980). A transcript of a trance induction with commentary. In E. Rossi (Ed.), *The collected papers of Milton H. Erickson on hypnosis. Vol. I. The nature of hypnosis and suggestion* (pp. 206–257). New York: Irvington.

Erickson, M., & Rossi, E. (1975/1980). Varieties of double bind. In E. Rossi (Ed.), *The collected papers of Milton H. Erickson on hypnosis. Vol. I. The nature of hypnosis and suggestion*. New York: Irvington.

Erickson, M., & Rossi, E. (1979). *Hypnotherapy: An exploratory casebook*. New York: Irvington.

Erickson, M. & Rossi, E. (1981). *Experiencing hypnosis: Therapeutic approaches to altered states*. New York: Irvington.

Erickson, M., Rossi, E., & Rossi, S. (1976). *Hypnotic realities*. New York: Irvington.

Haley, J. (Ed.) (1985). *Conversations with Milton H. Erickson, M.D. Vol I: Changing individuals; Vol. II: Changing couples; Vol. III: Changing children and families*. New York: Triangle.

Hammond, D. C. (1987). Book Reviews of Volumes I and II of "The seminars, workshops, and lectures of Milton H. Erickson." *American Journal of Clinical Hypnosis, 30*(2), 151–153.

Jung, C. (1979). *The collected works of Carl G. Jung. Vol. XX. General index*. Bollingen Series XX. Princeton, NJ: Princeton University Press.

Rossi, E., & Jichaku, P. (1983). Therapeutic and transpersonal double binds: Continuing the legacy of Gregory Bateson and Milton H. Erickson. In E. Rossi & M. Ryan (Eds.), *Creative choice in hypnosis. Vol. IV. The seminars, workshops, and lectures of Milton H. Erickson*. New York: Irvington.

Rossi, E., & Ryan, M. (Eds.) (1985). *Life reframing in hypnosis. Vol. II. The seminars, workshops, and lectures of Milton H. Erickson*. New York: Irvington.

Rossi, E., & Ryan, M. (Eds.) (1990). *Creative choice in hypnosis. Vol. IV. The seminars, workshops, and lectures of Milton H. Erickson*. New York: Irvington.

Structural Characteristics and Thematic Patterns of Interspersal Techniques of Milton H. Erickson: A Quantitative Analysis of the Case of Joe

Akira Otani

Erickson's interspersal approach as illustrated in the case of Joe was studied empiri-cally by frequency and correlational methods. The data indicate that the macrodynamics of interspersal techniques are comprised of two structural components: antecedent statements and indirect suggestions. This finding fully supports the two-level communication model expounded by Erickson and Rossi (1979). The study also identified a linear trend with three themes among the interspersal suggestions: trance induction, pain control, and illness coping. These findings are discussed with regard to utilization theory, and clinical implications are examined.

The interspersal technique is one of the most impressive, yet a little mystifying, approaches to trance induction and hypnotherapy developed by Milton H. Erickson. In his well-publicized case of Joe, Erickson (1966) demonstrated convincingly the clinical significance of this approach in working with this highly resistant, terminally ill patient.

The nature and forms of indirect suggestion composing the interspersal

The author gratefully acknowledges the research assistance of Ms. Pam Corbin and Maria K. Letras for the reliability assessment of the data. Ms. Debby Loomis and Ruth Roberts also provided invaluable help for the manuscript preparation and figure drawing. The author expresses his sincere gratitude to them. Address correspondence to: Akira Otani, Shoemaker Hall, University of Maryland, College Park, MD 20742-8111.

approach have been analyzed and discussed extensively by Erickson and his co-workers (Erickson & Rossi, 1979; 1981; Haley, 1973). In essence, Erickson (1966, p. 262; Erickson et al., 1976, p. 226) viewed the interspersal technique to consist of two components: 1) fixation of attention on the conscious level, followed by 2) appropriate suggestions to the unconscious. Because of these characteristics, the interspersal technique exemplifies a form of hypnotic two-level communication (Erickson & Rossi, 1976, p. 447).

Although this theoretical formulation of the mechanisms underlying the interspersal technique appears sound, no empirical evidence currently exists to support its validity. In order to understand the nature and process of this procedure more objectively, rigorous scientific investigation is warranted.

In the current study Erickson's original transcript with Joe was analyzed quantitatively to examine the following two questions.

1) What are the structural properties of Erickson's suggestions to Joe? To be more specific, what are the macrodynamics of the interspersal approach depicted in this case? The term *macrodynamics* refers to the various forms and sequential patterns of suggestion observed in trance induction and hypnotherapeutic process (Otani, 1989). Exploration of these dynamics can provide valuable information with regard to the two-level hypothesis of the interspersal technique.

2) What thematic patterns exist among Erickson's interspersal suggestions to Joe? Careful inspection of the transcript shows that Erickson skillfully combined several different *motifs* in his suggestions to Joe in order to gain therapeutic effects. Generally, hypnotic effects are accomplished by offering a variety of meaningful suggestions to a patient. Thus, in order to fully comprehend the therapeutic dimensions and mechanisms of the interspersal approach, the content of each suggestion and the thematic patterns of these suggestions need to be studied.

These two questions are critical in scientifically evaluating the nature of the Ericksonian interspersal approach to hypnosis. Once understood, the research findings should help clinical hypnotherapists and practitioners enhance their interspersal skills in their work.

Method

Materials

The verbatim transcript of the case of Joe (Erickson, 1966, pp. 269–271) was selected for the study. This case was chosen for three reasons: 1) it is one of, if not the, most famous case in which the interspersal approach was applied; 2) the transcript presents in detail the different forms of suggestion offered to the patient; and 3) Erickson provided his own commentaries about the case and the technique.

In conducting the analysis, a total of 37 interspersal suggestions, indicated by Erickson in italics in the text, were sampled. For each of the 37 suggestions, an "antecedent" statement was first identified. These statements consisted of phrases and sentences which preceded directly the suggestions in the text. As a result, this procedure generated 37 pairings of antecedent-suggestion units. To illustrate, one unit consisted of: "one puts a tomato seed in the ground" (antecedent) . . . "one can *feel hope*" (suggestion) (Erickson, 1966, p. 270).

These 37 pairs of antecedent-suggestion units were classified into different categories of suggestion, using the taxonomy developed by Erickson and Rossi (1980). These data were then analyzed statistically to study the macrodynamic characteristics of the interspersal approach (research question 1).

To investigate the thematic patterns among the interspersal suggestions (research question 2), the 37 suggestions were classified by their primary theme into one of three groups: 1) trance induction and facilitation (e.g., "I wish that you will *listen to me comfortably*"); 2) pain control and health promotion (e.g., "*You can't feel* it growing"); and 3) management and coping with the terminal illness (e.g., "It's so *nice to have food in one's stomach*"). In this way, the 37 suggestions were thematically categorized and coded by their intended theme in the order of appearance. The series of 37 numbers, ranging from 1 to 3, was then submitted to data analysis.

Data Reliability

In order to establish reliability of the data, two graduate students in Counseling and Human Development served as raters and analyzed the transcript independently. Both students were interested in learning trance induction techniques but were naive to the research hypotheses. They received a 2-hour didactic training on the forms and themes of suggestion prior to the data coding.

The average interrater reliability with the original coding, as measured by the phi coefficient, yielded .84 ($p < .001$) and .65 ($p < .01$) for research questions 1 and 2, respectively. Although probably inflated due to sampling error, these indexes indicate moderate to adequate reliability. Statistical properties of phi are discussed in Upton (1978).

Statistical Analysis

Since the numerical data in this study were categorical in nature, data analysis utilized classification and correlational techniques. For the first question investigating structural properties of the interspersal technique, the categorized suggestions in each dyad were analyzed by frequency and percentage count. The results were tabulated and diagrammed to assist interpretation.

The second question, which examined thematic trends among the interspersed suggestions, the 37 categorized codes were correlated with a sequence of numbers from 1 to 37, using the Pearson product-moment formula. To conduct this analysis, the three categorical themes were assumed to have an ordinal property. That is, the larger the categorized value becomes, the later the theme appears in the text. The obtained linear correlation coefficient was also checked against the nonlinear eta-squared statistic. This comparison was performed to test if the themes in the suggestions progressed in a "straight and steady" (linear) or more "irregular and oblique" (nonlinear) fashion. This procedure is described in Darlington and Carlson (1987, p. 141).

Results and Discussion

General Characteristics of Interspersal Approach

Structural Components. Categorical analysis of the 37 antecedent-suggestion units of interspersal suggestions showed nine different patterns among them. These results are summarized in Table 1. Of the

Table 1
Frequency and Percentage Count Analysis for the
Macrodynamics of the Interspersal Approach

RANKING	PATTERNS			FREQUENCY	PERCENTAGE (%)
1.	IAF	$\longrightarrow$	IMD	15	40.5
2.	IAF	$\longrightarrow$	IMP	5	13.6
3.	TRU	$\longrightarrow$	IMD	4	10.8
	IMD	$\longrightarrow$	IMD	4	10.8
4.	TRU	$\longrightarrow$	IMP	3	8.1
5.	IAF	$\longrightarrow$	DIR	2	5.4
	IMD	$\longrightarrow$	IMP	2	5.4
6.	TRU	$\longrightarrow$	DIR	1	2.7
7.	IMD	$\longrightarrow$	DIR	1	2.7
	Total			37	100.0

$\chi^2 = 148.86 \ (p < .001)$

NOTE: IAF = Indirect Associative Focusing; IMD = The Implied Directive; IMP = Implication; TRU = Truisms; DIR = Direct Suggestion nine sequences, the two most frequent patterns were Indirect Associative Focusing (IAF) in combination with one of the two forms of implied suggestion, namely, the Implied Directive (IMD) and Implication (IMP). These patterns jointly accounted for more than half (54%) of all interspersal suggestions in the text.

Two other less common patterns included an Implied Directive component. Truisms (TRU) related patterns, TRU-IMD and IMD-IMD combinations, each totaled roughly 11% of the 37 suggestions. The latter sequence is interesting in that it illustrates a repetition in Erickson's trance work (Erickson, 1959). The overall model yielded a statistically significant chi-square result ($p < .001$), suggesting these four patterns characterize the macrodynamics among the suggestions.

Note that all nine patterns of interspersal techniques consist of only five forms of hypnotic suggestion: IAF, IMD, IMP, TRU, and Direct Suggestion (DIR). These same components also characterized Erickson's more general approach to trance induction. In particular, the IAF-IMD sequence is one of the basic dynamics that signify Erickson's indirect style of hypnotherapy (Otani, 1989). These findings strongly support that the interspersal approach is structurally identical to other indirect approaches to hypnosis demonstrated by Erickson.

Figure 1 presents a schematic summary of the patterns among the five components. This diagram shows both major and minor patterns among the five components. It illuminates the integral role of the Implied Directive (IMD), supporting Erickson and Rossi's (1979) contention that subtle implication is an indispensable element in indirect approach.

Of the five components, IAF and TRU are considered to evoke various mental responses and to fixate the client's attention, while IMD, IMP, and DIR presumably serve to promote behavior change (Erickson & Rossi, 1979). In short, the combination of these two types of hypnotic suggestion may be the central macrodynamic mechanism underlying the interspersal approach. This process is indeed what Erickson and Rossi (1976, pp. 446–448; 1979, pp. 19–22) called "two-level communication."

To illustrate the above discussion, examine the following excerpts. "A luscious tomato sun-ripened" (IAF) . . . "*It's so nice to have food in one's stomach*" (IMD); "One puts a tomato seed in the ground" (TRU) . . . "One can *feel hope*" (IMD); and "I wonder if the tomato plant can" (IAF) . . . "*Joe, feel really feel a kind of comfort*" (DIR) (Erickson, 1966, pp. 270–271). Note that the hypnotic suggestion (italicized) in each of these examples follows a statement describing tomato plants. That is, each antecedent matches the client's frame of reference, which was that of a successful florist. It is easy to speculate that these antecedent statements elicited rich mental images and associations in Joe, accelerating his acceptance of the hypnotic suggestions.

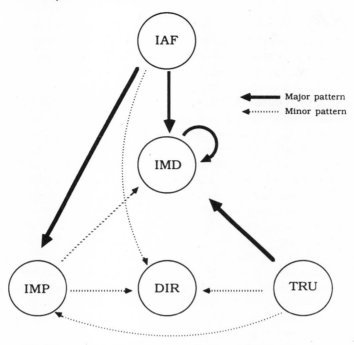

NOTE: IAF = Indirect Associative Focusing; IMD = The Implied Directive;
           IMP = Implication; DIR = Direct Suggestion; TRU = Truisms

Figure 1.   The macrodynamics of Erickson's interspersal suggestions to Joe.

From a theoretical standpoint, this use of the client's own inner resources categorizes interspersal approach as a special form of the *utilization approach*. This finding should not be too surprising. As Erickson (Erickson et al., 1976, p. 29) stated, "You always use the patient's own words and experience as much as possible for trance induction and suggestion." The interspersal approach reflects this principle well.

In summation, the interspersal approach to hypnosis structurally consists of two steps: 1) facilitating conscious/unconscious response via "stimulus" words or phrases to secure the client's attention, and 2) offering direct and/or indirect suggestions to achieve desired therapeutic goals. Because the interspersal approach makes full use of the client's rich inner resources, it should be viewed as a form of the utilization approach.

Thematic Patterns.   Thematic trends among Erickson's suggestions to Joe were assessed by correlational analysis. The degree of linear association between the three topical categories of suggestion and the series of 37 numbers yielded .82 ($p < .001$). This sizable, statistically significant result reveals an implicit order in Erickson's remarks to Joe. The magnitude of the association also suggests that Erickson interspersed the therapeutic directives in the sequence of 1) trance induction, 2) pain control, and 3) illness coping.

To test this hypothesis further, the eta-squared statistic was calculated and examined. Unlike the Pearson's product-moment correlation coefficient, this measure expresses a degree of nonlinear relationship between two sets. Hence, a comparison of these two statistics indicates a linear and nonlinear distinction of the observed relationship between the themes and the order of the interspersed suggestions. The eta-squared formula yielded an index of .72 for the sample used. The minimum discrepancy between the squared correlation coefficient and the eta-squared index ($.72 - .82^2 = .04$) supports the contention that Erickson's interspersal suggestions were approximately linear in nature in this example.

Translating into a nonmathematical language, this linear trend means Erickson proceeded steadily and systematically from general to more specific topics in the course of his interspersal hypnotherapy session with Joe. Consider the following successive examples: "I wish that you will *listen to me* comfortably . . . It makes one *curious* . . . *You can listen to me, Joe* . . . *You can keep on listening, wondering, just wondering what you can really learn* [trance induction suggestions] . . . And then *you can't see* it growing . . . *you can't feel* it growing . . . *Joe, feel really feel a kind of comfort* . . . Would such a plant *have nice feelings, a sense of comfort* [pain control suggestions] . . . So *full of promise to give you the desire to eat* . . . It's so *nice to have food in one's stomach* . . . A thirsty child has and can *want a drink,* Joe . . . *Sleep so restfully, so comfortably* [illness-coping suggestions]." (Erickson 1966, pp. 270–271).

In this excerpt notice Erickson painstakingly established Joe's mental set toward hypnotic learning and trance induction *before* dealing with the patient's carcinogenic pain. Similarly, Erickson gave illness-coping directives, such as food intake and drinking, *only after* relief from pain and physical comfort were suggested. The above example elegantly demonstrates Erickson's expert sequential blending of the different themes in his communication with the patient.

Recently, Zeig (1987) published Erickson's own account of the interspersal techniques in this case:

> I started as far away from Joe's cancer as I could, without trying to identify it. Indeed, I said a lot of words that Joe translated into the experiential learnings that he thought he had lost forever until he had built up a sufficient supply of his good associations to replace the things that he didn't want. (p. 253)

This quote corroborates the contention that Erickson planned the suggestion sequence, which began with distant topics and approached the key issues successively. The empirical analysis confirms his assertion.

Clinical Implications

Advantages of the Approach

Clinical interpretation of these statistical findings needs caution, since Erickson (1958, p. 175) emphasized that suggestions need to be tailored for each individual. Erickson, without doubt, chose "tomato plants" for Joe because of the patient's floral background and interest. Hence, without further replication using different data, the current findings are limited in terms of their generalizability. Nevertheless, the general macrodynamics characterizing the interspersal approach deserve careful attention of clinicians.

There are two major advantages in using interspersal strategies in psychotherapy. First, *this technique minimizes client resistance.* As mentioned earlier, the interspersal approach fixates the client's conscious mind by means of relevant antecedent statements while offering hypnotic directives immediately thereafter. In doing so, the therapist fully utilizes the client's frame of reference by carefully selecting the antecedent topics to access internal associations. Little wonder that these mechanisms effectively and potently curtail the client's resistance to therapeutic suggestions. Remember that Joe was initially so defensive that he "disliked even the mention of the word *hypnosis*" (italics original) (Erickson, 1966, p. 268). Interspersed suggestions successfully bypassed his resistance and took effect because of Erickson's calculated use of attention-catching antecedents and target hypnotic directives.

In addition to resistance management, the second distinct advantage of the interspersal approach is that *the therapeutic results tend to be thorough and gratifying.* As Erickson (1948) pointed out, the ultimate goal of psychotherapy lies in "a reassociation, an elaboration, a reorganization, and an integration of [one's] experiential life" (p. 43). It is for this reason that he advocated the utilization of clients' inner resources and indirect suggestions in therapy. The interspersal approach models this principle well.

The macrodynamic analysis shows that the interspersal approach combines utilization and indirection structurally (i.e., IAF, TRU $\longrightarrow$ IMD, IMP). This evidence warrants that *if properly applied,* this approach can produce highly favorable therapeutic outcome. Indeed, many of Erickson's cases present excellent examples illustrating his mastery of this macrodynamic principle (see Erickson, 1980; Haley, 1973). Interested clinicians are encouraged to study the interspersal macrodynamics among some of the cases.

Practical Guidelines

The experimental data in this study suggest the following heuristic guidelines for clinical implementation of interspersal techniques in trance induction and hypnotherapeutic work.

1. *Study and Use the Client's Experiential Framework.* Experiential framework refers to the background, life experience and style, values, hobbies, and other unique characteristics of the client. These types of information are indispensable in the clinical application of interspersal suggestion. As demonstrated earlier, they can stimulate the client's unconscious associative patterns to create a favorable therapeutic climate. In this sense, the mastery of interspersal skills starts with learning to observe, gather, and understand unique facts about the client. Once identified, the clinician should use the client's experiential framework by offering appropriate *Indirect Associative Focusing* (IAF) and *Truisms* (TRU) forms of suggestion (Erickson & Rossi, 1979).

2. *Master Ways to Offer Suggestions Indirectly.* Erickson and Rossi (1979) viewed implication as one of the most fundamental, yet potent elements of hypnotic communication. "With implication," they wrote, "and all other forms of indirect suggestion, we are presuming to [be] making an effort that will create and facilitate the actual unconscious processes that will create the desired response" (p. 39). As they suggested, a clinician will benefit from learning various ways and forms of indirect suggestion. To be specific, the macrodynamic analysis in Figure 1 shows that both *Implication* (IMP) and the *Implied Directive* (IMD) following the IAF play principal roles in the interspersal approach. These two forms of suggestion thus deserve special attention when studying interspersal techniques.

3. *Sharpen Up Linguistic Sensitivity and Vocal Control.* Careful analysis of Erickson's (1976–1978, p. 489; Erickson & Rossi, 1981, p. 26) writing reveals that he frequently interspersed suggestions by manipulating his words (e.g., multiple meanings, puns, pauses) as well as his vocal cues (e.g., pitch, tone, intonation). To paraphrase Zeig (1987, p. 392), an effective therapist is not necessarily the one who communicates meaningful ideas; rather, he/she is the one who communicates ideas meaningfully. Commenting upon his expert use of vocal cues in trance induction, Erickson (Erickson & Rossi, 1976, p. 438) said, "Yes, the phrase to the unconscious is spoken softly . . . I use one tone of voice to speak to the conscious mind and another to speak to the unconscious." A clinician

hence needs to develop keen linguistic sensitivity and to master vocal control when offering suggestions while using interspersal techniques.

4. *Investigate and Incorporate Micro- and Macrodynamic Principles When Designing Interspersal Suggestions.* The research results indicate that although inconspicuous, Erickson's interspersal suggestions to Joe were carefully sequenced according to specific themes. This finding means that a clinician needs to identify necessary themes for each client and arrange them in an appropriate order in performing interspersal techniques. Conversely, failure to discover and organize therapeutic themes will most likely mitigate the therapeutic effect.

From a pragmatic standpoint, construction of well-organized interspersal suggestions should incorporate microdynamic as well as macrodynamic principles of trance induction. The nature and characteristics of these principles are described in Erickson and Rossi (1976, 1979) and Otani (1989), respectively. Remember, Erickson wrote down all suggestions in advance in order to study the art of hypnosis (Erickson & Rossi, 1976–1978).

Conclusion

The experimental findings of the current study reveal that Erickson's interspersal suggestions to Joe consisted of five forms of suggestion. There was a linear progression of themes among the hypnotic directives. The macrodynamics of the interspersal approach support Erickson and Rossi's two-level communication hypothesis of the interspersal approach. Since the research analyzed only one case, replication of the study with other cases is imperative. Meanwhile, clinicians are encouraged to apply these principles in their practice.

References

Darlington, R. B., & Carlson, P. M. (1987). *Behavioral statistics: Logic and methods.* New York: Free Press.

Erickson, M. H. (1948). Hypnotic psychotherapy. In E. L. Rossi (Ed.), *The collected papers of Milton H. Erickson on hypnosis: Vol. I. The nature of hypnosis and suggestion* (pp. 168–176). New York: Irvington.

Erickson, M. H. (1958). Naturalistic techniques of hypnosis. In E. L. Rossi (Ed.), *The collected papers of Milton H. Erickson on hypnosis: Vol. IV. Innovative hypnotherapy* (pp. 35–48). New York: Irvington.

Erickson, M. H. (1959). Hypnosis in painful terminal illness. In E. L. Rossi (Ed.), *The collected papers of Milton H. Erickson on hypnosis: Vol. IV. Innovative hypnotherapy* (pp. 255–261). New York: Irvington.

Erickson, M. H. (1966). The interspersal hypnotic technique for symptom correction and pain control. In E. L. Rossi (Ed.), *The collected papers of Milton H.*

Erickson on hypnosis: Vol. IV. Innovative hypnotherapy (pp. 262–278). New York: Irvington.

Erickson, M. H. (1980). *The collected papers of Milton H. Erickson on hypnosis: Vol. IV. Innovative hypnotherapy* (E. L. Rossi, Ed.). New York: Irvington.

Erickson, M. H., & Rossi, E. L. (1976). Two-level communication and the microdynamics of trance and suggestion. In E. L. Rossi (Ed.). *The collected papers of Milton H. Erickson on hypnosis: Vol I. The nature of hypnosis and suggestion* (pp. 430–451). New York: Irvington.

Erickson, M. H., & Rossi, E. L. (1976–78). Indirect forms of suggestion in hand levitation. In E. L. Rossi (Ed.), *The collected papers of Milton H. Erickson on hypnosis: Vol. I. The nature of hypnosis and suggestion* (pp. 478–490). New York: Irvington.

Erickson, M. H., & Rossi, E. L. (1979). *Hypnotherapy: An exploratory casebook.* New York: Irvington.

Erickson, M. H., & Rossi, E. L. (1980). The indirect forms of suggestion. In E. L. Rossi (Ed.), *The collected papers of Milton H. Erickson on hypnosis: Vol. I. The nature of hypnosis and suggestion* (pp. 452–477). New York: Irvington.

Erickson, M. H., & Rossi, E. L. (1981). *Experiencing hypnosis: Therapeutic approaches to altered states.* New York: Irvington.

Erickson, M. H., Rossi, E. L., & Rossi, S. I. (1976). *Hypnotic realities: The induction of clinical hypnosis and forms of indirect suggestion.* New York: Irvington.

Haley, J. (1973). *Uncommon therapy: The psychiatric techniques of Milton H. Erickson, M.D.* New York: Norton.

Otani, A. (1989). An empirical investigation of Milton H. Erickson's approach to trance induction: A Markov chain analysis of two published cases. In S. R. Lankton (Ed.), *Ericksonian hypnosis: Application, preparation and research* (Ericksonian Monographs 5).

Upton, G. J. G. (1978). *The analysis of cross-tabulated data.* New York: Wiley.

Zeig, J. K. (1987). Therapeutic patterns of Ericksonian influence communication. In J. K. Zeig (Ed.), *The evolution of psychotherapy.* New York: Brunner/Mazel.

An Experimental and Qualitative Evaluation of an Ericksonian Hypnotic Intervention for Family Relationship Problems

William R. Nugent, Ph.D.

An experimental and qualitative study of an Ericksonian hypnotic approach used in a clinical application is described. The subject of the study was a 40-year-old woman. The dependent variable was a measure of the level of angry, defensive responses made by the woman to two family members, her husband and her teenage daughter. Also included as dependent variables were scores on Hudson's Index of Marital Satisfaction and Index of Parental Attitudes. The independent variable was a hypnotic procedure designed using methods that fall under the rubric "Ericksonian hypnotic procedures." A multiple baseline single subject design was used to investigate experimentally the causal effect of the intervention procedure on the dependent variable. Qualitative descriptions of the apparent effects of the intervention procedure were also gathered from the client in several clinical interviews and through use of an open-ended questionnaire. The possible use of this type of procedure as an adjunct method in marital and family therapy is discussed.

Several clinical investigations of Ericksonian hypnotic procedures have been carried out recently. A number of these have provided evidence suggesting causal effects of Ericksonian hypnotic methods for clinical use with anxiety disorders (Nugent, 1988a). Another experimental study provided evidence for the causal efficacy of an Ericksonian hypnotic intervention for changing the performance behavior of an athlete (Nugent, 1988b). There are also some relatively strong case study data supportive of the causal efficacy of Ericksonian hypnotic approaches with

Address correspondence to: William R. Nugent, Ph.D., 3238 Citation Trail, Tallahassee, FL 32308 needle phobias, sleep disturbance, and claustrophobic responses (Nugent, 1989a; Nugent et al., 1984). While these studies provide some empirical evidence suggesting causal effects of Ericksonian hypnotic procedures, further clinical experiments are needed to provide a sound empirical base for the use of Erickson's clinical methods.

While experimental methods can powerfully suggest causality, qualitative methods provide important descriptive information, such as of an individual's peculiar subjective experience of a clinical intervention (Patton, 1980). Such descriptions can be used in the development and clear explication of concepts. They can also, when integrated with experimental methods, provide a means of focusing upon an evaluation research question that complements experimental results; this multimethodological means of approaching a research question is called "triangulation" (Patton, 1980).

This paper describes an experimental and qualitative study of an Ericksonian hypnotic intervention, carried out in a clinical setting, used to change aspects of relationship difficulties in a family. The single case experimental analysis of the intervention procedure will be described. Then, a qualitative analysis of the intervention and its effects will be presented, followed by an integration of the results of the two methodological approaches.

Methodology

Subject

The subject of this clinical study was a 40-year-old female. This woman was married and had two children, a 16-year-old girl (who will be referred to as D) and an 18-year-old boy (who will be referred to as S). Both the woman and her husband were college graduates, and the woman held a master's degree. She worked in a private practice, while her husband worked in a hospital setting. The daughter was a high-school junior, the son a freshman in college.

Qualitative Description of Target Problem

The woman had been experiencing relationship problems with both her husband and her daughter for several years. The woman described her relationship with her husband (H) as seriously problematic and stated that she remained married to him "primarily for the kids" (phrases in quotes are direct statements from the client taken from clinical interviews and/or client comments on an open-ended evaluation form). She stated that she had "lost all trust in him" and that she had "gunnysacked over the years" a lot of resentment that prevented her from wanting to work on her marital relationship in any significant way. She strongly resisted any suggestions that she and her husband come in for treatment together.

The woman's presenting concern was her relationship with her daughter. This relationship had, apparently, been "deteriorating for 3 or 4 years" and had been "much worse for about a year." The woman was concerned that "irreparable harm may be happening to the relationship" between her and D. Specifically, the woman and D had been having interchanges, "consistently for approximately a year," in which the client would "become provoked and act like an angry child." In these interchanges, the woman would respond to "provocative" stimuli from D with "yelling, profanity, pouting, crying, criticism, and verbal abuse." She also responded with "feelings of frustration, feelings of anger at a level that was inappropriate to the situation, and a feeling of not being valued as an authority figure." D's behaviors that evoked these responses included "rolling her eyes when asked to do something, interrupting me, not obeying within a reasonable period of time, and not letting a subject drop after she has been given an explanation when she has been told 'no'."

These interchanges, though not particularly frequent in occurrence, were "so negative" in character, resulting in such angry bitter feelings, that she feared their continuation would permanently damage her relationship with D. The woman had been unable on her own to make changes in this interactional pattern.

The woman reported that a very similar pattern of interaction transpired between her and her husband. H would do something such as "telling me my actions are stupid, doing things he *knows* annoy me, not answering me when I ask a question or make a statement." Her response to H would be characterized by the same behaviors and feelings with which she responded to provocative stimuli from her daughter. This pattern with H had "been a problem on and off during the entire time we have been married." However, this problematic pattern had been "consistently a problem for me for about 5 years."

The woman described her relationship with her son as being "real good." She described him as being "wonderful . . . a great person to get along with." She reported no problems in this relationship.

The woman was very resistant to bringing in her daughter or husband for relationship work. She preferred working individually with the therapist. She readily accepted the proposal to use a hypnotic approach, though she was reluctant for any therapeutic intervention in her relationship with her husband. However, she agreed to work on the problematic interchange with him provided it could be done without requiring her to "feel any of the bad painful feelings again that I've felt with him before."

Dependent Variables

There were three dependent variables in this experiment: 1) scores on a self-anchored scale (Bloom & Fischer, 1982, chapter 7) measuring the type of response the woman made to "Provocative stimuli" from H, D, and/or S; 2) scores on Hudson's Index of Parental Attitudes (IPA); and 3) scores on Hudson's Index of Marital Satisfaction (IMS) (Bloom & Fischer, 1982; Corcoran & Fischer, 1987; Fischer, 1978; Hudson, 1982; Hudson et al., 1980).

The self-anchored scale measured the level of response the woman made to her daughter, to her husband, or to her son whenever one of them manifested "provocative" verbal and/or nonverbal behavior. Scores on this scale, developed using procedures described in Bloom and Fischer (1982, chapter 7), ranged from –10 to +10. The major anchor points (Bloom & Fischer, 1982, pp. 170–175) on this scale were set such that a –10 indicated the worst possible response—a response characterized by totally uncontrolled cursing, yelling, and feelings of anger on the part of the client. A +10 on this scale indicated the most positive response possible—a response characterized by no yelling or cursing at all, the client listening carefully to H, D, or S, the client clearly expressing her feelings and desires in a nonattacking manner, and no angry feelings on the part of the client. A 0 on this scale indicated a point half-way between –10 and +10.

The woman carried around with her a 3 x 5 index card and self-rated her level of response to any provocative stimuli from her daughter, son, or husband. The *arithmetic average* of the woman's responses to provocative stimuli over a measurement period was used as an indicator of the overall level of the problematic interactions during that specific interval.

Few studies have focused upon the reliability and validity of self-anchored scales such as the one used in this study. Evidence bearing on the psychometric properties of self-anchored type scales has been provided by a number of authors (Farkas et al., 1979; Nugent, 1989b; Thyer et al., 1984; Wincze et al., 1977). These studies suggest self-anchored type scales can have good psychometric characteristics.

The Index of Parental Attitudes (IPA), used as a second dependent measure in this study, is a 25-item Likert-type scale (with scores ranging from 0 to 100; higher scores indicate problems of greater severity), which "is completed by a parent with respect to the parent's relationship with a specific child. It measures the degree, severity, or magnitude of a problem the parent has in the relationship with a child—regardless of the age of the child." (Hudson, 1982, p. 5). Scores above 30 have empirical evidence as being indicative of a clinically significant parent-child relationship problem (Hudson, 1982). Hudson reports a coefficient alpha reliability of

.97 for the IPA, with a standard error of measurement of 3.64. Hudson also reports that the IPA has excellent validity characteristics.[1]

The Index of Marital Satisfaction (IMS), also a 25-item Likert-type scale (with scores ranging from 0 to 100; higher scores indicate problems of greater severity), is "designed to measure the degree, severity, or magnitude of a problem a spouse or partner has in the marital relationship. The IMS does not measure or characterize the dyadic relationship as a single entity but measures the magnitude of marital discord or dissatisfaction that is felt or perceived by one partner" (Hudson, 1982, p. 4). Again, scores above 30 are indicative of clinically significant levels of marital discord (Hudson, 1982). Hudson reports the coefficient alpha reliability of the IMS as being .96, with a standard error of measurement of 4.00. Hudson also reports evidence of excellent validity characteristics for the IMS. The IMS was used as a third dependent measure in this study.[2]

Treatment Variable

Numerous writers have discussed Erickson's *utilization model* (Erickson & Rossi, 1979; Gilligan, 1987; Lankton & Lankton, 1983). This model states essentially that hypnotic procedures may be used to move *personal resources*, imbedded in a nonproblematic context, into problematic personal, interpersonal, and/or social contexts. Personal resources may be conceptualized as any physical, cognitive, and/or affective ability or experience the person has in her/his past. These resources are accessed and focused, through use of indirect suggestion, upon self-directed change that is carried out unconsciously via autonomous mental processes.[3]

A sequence of indirect hypnotic suggestions was written out on paper. These suggestions were focused upon the woman: 1) searching unconsciously for personal resources appropriate for problematic interpersonal contexts (the client perceiving "provocative" behavior) with a specified person (daughter or husband); and 2) unconsciously determining how she would use these resources in appropriate problematic interpersonal contexts (when either daughter or husband engaged in "provocative" behavior).

This sequence of suggestions was to be read directly to the woman as part of the following series of steps. First, the therapist engaged in a discussion with the woman of the ability of the unconscious mind to solve problems without conscious awareness. Examples of this process were given. Then, a progressive relaxation induction method was to be used to induce trance. "Trance" was defined as the woman showing three or more of the common behavioral indicators of trance described by Erickson and

Rossi (1979). The sequence of suggestions was to be read directly from the prepared sheet to the woman while she was in trance. The verbatim series of suggestions used can be seen in the Appendix.

Thus, the treatment variable was defined as the set of steps: (a) pretrance discussion of the abilities of the unconscious mind to solve problems without conscious awareness; (b) use of a progressive relaxation procedure to induce trance; and (c) upon the woman showing three or more of the behaviors defined by Erickson and Rossi (1979) as common indicators of trance, reading the sequence of suggestions shown in the Appendix.

Experimental Design

A multiple baseline across behaviors, single case design was used in this study (Bloom & Fischer, 1982). After construction of the self-anchored scale, a visual representation of it was made (similar to Figure 1) and was used to gather a retrospective baseline, phase A_r, (Bloom & Fischer, 1982; Campbell & Stanley, 1963; Hudson, 1982; Isaac & Michael, 1971) on the woman's levels of response to provocative stimuli from daughter, son, and husband during the preceding 2 months.[4] The woman also self-recorded her levels of response to provocative stimuli from D, H, and S for 1 week, producing data for a concurrent baseline, phase A_c. The woman continued to self-record the level of her responses to "provocative" stimuli from D, H, and S throughout the course of this study. The exact sequence of measurement can be seen in Figure 1. The woman also filled out the IMS and IPA (once focusing on her relationship with D and once on her relationship with S) at several points during this study, as shown in Figure 2.

The hypnotic intervention described above was first carried out with a focus on the client's responses to provocative stimuli from D. Four weeks after this intervention (see Figures 1 and 2), the hypnotic intervention was carried out with a focus upon her responses to H. Before this intervention, the woman expressed severe misgivings about attempting to change her relationship with her husband; she expressed concern that the intervention would uncover uncomfortable feelings and leave her vulnerable to him. In response to these concerns, the therapist assured the woman that her unconscious would take care of her and made the clinical decision to alter the planned intervention. Instead of reading the prepared series of indirect suggestions, after inducing trance via the progressive relaxation approach, the therapist employed the following series of indirect suggestions:

> Your unconscious can review the problematic situations you
> encounter with your husband . . . and can review all your abilities

and experiences . . . just like you did for D . . . to find just those abilities and resources you need in order to respond to provocative stimuli from him in new ways . . . ways that will fully meet your needs as a person . . . ways that will make you feel good about yourself. Your unconscious can think about these things . . . without your conscious awareness . . . the rest of the day . . . and tonight . . . and you need not make any changes until you are really ready. As soon as your unconscious knows that you will do these things . . . you can spontaneously awaken from trance.

The woman returned the next week and a second intervention session was carried out. In this session, the original planned intervention, described previously, in the section on the treatment variable, was carried out exactly as in the first intervention session except the focus was upon her responses to her husband instead of to her daughter. No further intervention sessions were used during the course of this experiment.

During subsequent sessions, measures of the dependent variables were taken and qualitative interviews were conducted, as described below. Two months after termination of clinical contact with the woman, a follow-up interview was conducted, in which measurements on all dependent variables were made.

Qualitative Design and Implementation

Qualitative data were gathered through two methods: open-ended conversational interviews and an open-ended questionnaire (Patton, 1980). Interviews were conducted both prior to beginning treatment, with a focus upon the nature of the problem, and 2 weeks following an intervention session, with a focus upon the relationship targeted by the intervention. Two months after completion of the experiment, a follow-up interview was conducted and the woman filled out the standardized open-ended questionnaire.

Results

Experimental Results

The results of the experiment are shown in Figures 1 and 2. Figure 1 shows the self-anchored scale data, while Figure 2 shows the IPA and IMS data.

The self-anchored scale data for the woman's interactions with her daughter, to the extent the woman's retrospective estimates are reliable, show a stable pattern of negative-level interactions prior to intervention. The concurrent baseline data for the woman's responses to D also show negative-level interactions. These self-anchored data show a change to

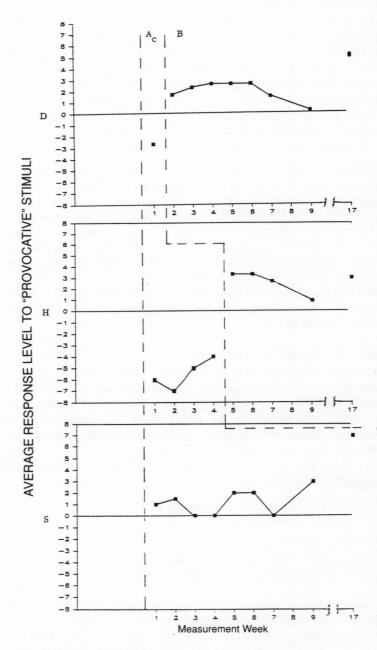

Figure 1:   Multiple Baseline Self-Anchored Scale Data.

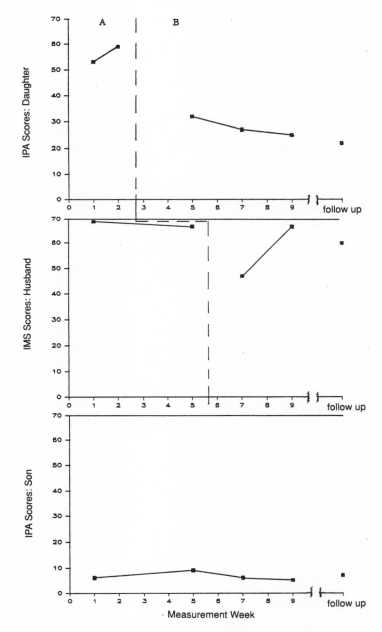

Figure 2:   Multiple Baseline Data on Index of Parental Attitudes (IPA) and Index of Marital Satisfaction (IMS).

positive-level interactions across the A–B phase change (namely, immediately following application of the treatment variable). The B phase data show a stable, essentially nonchanging level for the postintervention period. There is a substantial improvement at follow-up.

The self-anchored scale data on the woman's responses to her husband show a negative level, with a slight trend in an improving direction across a 4-week concurrent baseline condition. The woman claimed in several interviews that interactions with her husband had been at a negative level, for "5 years, maybe more." The baseline data clearly show a standing pattern of negative-level responses to provocative stimuli from the husband. This negative level changes abruptly to a positive level across the A–B phase change. This positive level of responses remains positive and stable, with a small deterioration at the week 9 measurement, throughout the remainder of the experiment. The deterioration at week 9 seems to have been heavily influenced by a bad fight that the woman had had with her husband. The woman rated her response to her husband during this fight at a –4. All other self-ratings during this measurement period were positive (the average without this influential data point being 2.5). This deterioration vanishes at follow-up.

The self-anchored data for the woman's responses to her son show a relatively stable level from retrospective baseline throughout the weeks of the concurrent baseline. There is a substantial improvement at follow-up.

The IPA data for the daughter show concurrent baseline levels of 55 and 59, indicative of a moderate-to-serious problem in the mother-daughter relationship (Hudson, personal communication, June 1986). This level drops across the A–B phase change to 32, a point suggesting the across-phase change may be clinically significant. The IPA scores show continuing, though small, decreases across the remaining measurements.

The IMS scores show a stable concurrent baseline level across two measurements (69 and 67). These scores are indicative of a fairly serious marital problem (Hudson, personal communication, June 1986). The IMS score drops, across the A–B phase change, to 47, a score indicative of a moderate-level marital problem (Hudson, personal communication, June 1986). The IMS score rises to 67 at the next measurement, and drops to 60 at follow-up.

During the course of the entire study the IPA scores for the woman's relationship with her son remained essentially stable at clinically trivial levels (between 6 and 9).

The across-phase changes in IPA and IMS scores are of clinical importance. The IPA scores drop to clinically nonsignificant levels. The IMS scores drop from serious to moderate levels. Further, both changes seem to occur concomitant with implementation of treatment focused upon the relevant relationship. The standardized scale data are also consistent with the self-anchored scale data. Both suggest that important changes occurred in relatively stable relationship states concomitant with application of the Ericksonian hypnotic intervention procedures.

Methodological Limitations of Results

These changes in dependent variable levels need to be considered within the context of some methodological limitations. First, the self-anchored scale concurrent baseline data for the woman's response to her daughter consist of a single data point, covering a span of 1 week. A longer baseline period, with more data points and stable dependent variable levels, would provide a more sound basis for causal inference in this study. A single baseline data point, while clinically justifiable, is methodologically weak (Thomas, 1978). Further, the use of retrospective data to establish baseline levels and trends is methodologically weak, leaving open the question of reliability (see reference note 5). Indeed, the reliability of the self-anchored scale data as a set is open to question, since there is no currently accepted means of assessing the reliability of the self-anchored scale used in this study. While some studies have suggested such measurement procedures can have good reliability characteristics, the reliability of the self-anchored data in this study cannot be determined.

The convergence of results of the data on the IPA and IMS, scales having relatively established psychometric properties, with the self-anchored scale data help off-set the foregoing methodological problems. The IPA and IMS baselines show relative stability, though those for responses to daughter and husband contain only two data points. Larger numbers of data points in baseline phase would have provided greater methodological rigor.

Qualitative Results

The woman described her experience of trance, in a response to a question on the open-ended questionnaire, as including "a decreased perception of time . . . decreased perception of external noises . . . feelings of heaviness . . . decreased perceptions of where my hands and arms were in relation to my body or the chair . . . [and] occasionally a sense of floating." These descriptions are consistent with the descriptions of trance given by Erickson and Rossi (1979), Lankton and Lankton (1983), and Gilligan (1987).

The woman described her interactions with her daughter and husband as being different after the intervention had been implemented. Immediately after the intervention had been implemented with a focus upon the woman's interactions with her daughter, the woman "drove home feeling kind of spacey." She spent the evening "feeling vulnerable, and as if I were preoccupied with something, but not knowing what it was, as if I were thinking about something, without knowing what I was thinking about."

This "vulnerability" and "preoccupation" were gone the next morning. She then felt "different" when her daughter manifested a "provocative" stimulus: "I feel somehow more aware. I can't say how I am more aware; it's just a feeling I have." This feeling of greater "awareness," according to the woman, seemed to open up different response options. She would respond differently to her daughter's "provocative" voice and/or "looks." There was "less yelling and verbal abuse towards her, more patience, increased ability to say 'no' and not get hooked into a debate, increased ability to have fun with her and emphasize her uniqueness and talents." The woman attributed these changes, in the open-ended questionnaire, to the hypnotic intervention, writing that the intervention "increased my ability to draw on the adult, rational part of myself and decrease the inappropriate, acting-out child part of myself."

At this point, the woman described no changes in her interactions with her husband. Immediately prior to use of the intervention focused upon her interactions with her husband, she had grave misgivings about its implementation and expressed concern that she would "feel again all the hurt and pain I have felt before." In implementing the intervention, the therapist had to put great emphasis on the way that the unconscious could creatively initiate changes in ways that would give her the emotional protection that she wanted. She agreed to the intervention being implemented after this framing of the procedure's effects.

After the intervention had been implemented, with the focus upon her interactions with her husband, the woman again described leaving and "driving home feeling kind of spacey and preoccupied." She again spent the evening "feeling vulnerable and preoccupied, but not knowing what I was preoccupied with." She then began to feel "less vulnerable . . . somehow emotionally safer" around her husband. She also began to respond differently to "provocative" stimuli from him. The "adult" in her seemed to be more in control when she responded to him, though the "child" was still there. She described the changes she experienced, in a response on the open-ended questionnaire: "I am less likely to take his 'abuse' personally and now have a higher opinion of myself [increased sense of personal value]. My responses are similar to the changes with [daughter]—less yelling, crying, pouting, and verbal attacks." She told the therapist, "I am very pleased at how I feel now around him. Rather than feeling more pain, I feel safer and less vulnerable. I feel so much better than I did before."

At the follow-up interview, the woman described the changes as having continued and further developed. She was "very pleased at how well things have been going. Home is a much better place to be now." The qualitative data all suggest that the woman experienced a positive subjective response to the intervention procedure.

Discussion and Conclusion

The results of this study, both experimental and qualitative, suggest that the hypnotic procedure *may* have caused the changes observed and discussed above. The triangulation on the effects of the interventions provided by the multiple dependent measures (self-anchored scale *and* standardized scales) and the mixed experimental/qualitative methodology all seem to converge toward this conclusion.

The first intervention session seems to have brought about a rather substantial change in the woman's relationship with her daughter, a change that generalized across time. Indeed, the change, according to Hudson's criteria, would seem to be from a moderate-to-severe relationship problem to a clinically nonsignificant problem.

The second intervention session seems to have brought about an important change in the woman's marital relationship, a change from a severe-level problem to a moderate-level problem (using Hudson's criteria). However, this change does not appear to have generalized across time. Apparently, the intervention effects were limited enough so as to be canceled out by other detrimental relationship patterns. Further, the *second* intervention session focused upon the woman's relationship with her husband appears to have had no effect upon her responses to him. The use of the intervention procedure apparently produced no changes subsequent to those occurring after the first session focused upon the client's responses to her husband.

This latter observation raises some question about the "active ingredients" in the intervention sessions. The exact indirect suggestions used in the two sessions, which seemed to initiate change, are different. Thus, the two apparently active intervention sessions are different, at least at the level of specific indirect suggestions given during trance. It might be argued that this change in specific indirect suggestions leaves this study open to claims that the indirect suggestions given during trance were not "active ingredients," that the mere act of performing a procedure called "hypnosis" initiated some type of placebo response. Given the design of this study, there is no way of ruling out such a possibility. Indeed, even if the same set of indirect suggestions had been used in both change-inducing sessions, this threat to the construct validity of the intervention used could not be ruled out on design arguments alone.

At least three possibilities present themselves as explanations for the observed change: 1) The mere use of an intervention labeled "hypnosis" initiated the change, via a placebo effect, without any specific effects due to "Ericksonian" components. 2) The use of the pretrance discussion of unconscious processes initiated a process activated by the use of a "trance induction" procedure, a process that would have caused change regardless of the specific indirect suggestions given during trance. 3) The specific indirect suggestions used during trance did play some role in the observed change. Unfortunately, there is no way the design used allows an unambiguous determination of which of these cases was operative in this study. Regardless of which of the above mechanisms was operative, the study clearly suggests that clinical procedures labeled "hypnotic" may have causal impact upon targets of change. Further, if either of the latter two explanations were the operative intervention mechanism, the study lends support to Erickson's clinical intervention models.

The changes in the woman's responses to and relationships with daughter and husband suggest that Ericksonian hypnotic interventions *may* be useful change-inducing methods for family therapy. The intervention procedures seem to have had significant impact upon the mother-daughter relationship, and a somewhat lesser impact upon the marital dyad. The effects that these changes will have across time upon the family system can only be speculated. The results of this study support the use of Ericksonian hypnotic methods in family therapy, even if the mere use of "hypnotic" procedures was the operative mechanism.

The qualitative descriptions given by the woman are consistent with Erickson's model of autonomous, self-directed unconscious change. The woman's descriptions suggest some process occurring within her that she was consciously aware of *only* at the occurrence/nonoccurrence level; she knew something was happening, but was unaware of exactly what was occurring. She described a sense of "preoccupation" with something, but a lack of awareness of what the preoccupation was with. These descriptions clearly suggest some mental process occurring largely outside of conscious volition, direction, and awareness.

The woman's descriptions of the changes are also consistent with Erickson's view that the unconscious can initiate changes in a manner that protects the individual's "conscious" personality. The woman had expressed strong concern and reluctance about any intervention focused upon her relationship with her husband. She was concerned about feeling further pain. However, it appears that the intervention resulted in the woman being able to change her responses to her husband in a manner honoring her conscious level concerns and needs. After the intervention she began to feel less vulnerable to her husband's "provocative" stimuli, feeling less pain instead of more.

Finally, the woman's qualitative descriptions are also consistent with Erickson's conceptualization of personal resources being made available from one context to a new context. While none of the woman's descriptions clearly detail a subjective sense of some unconscious shuffling of inner resources, they are nonetheless consistent with such a model. Indeed, reading through the indirect suggestions used in the intervention sessions reveals a focus upon the reshuffling of inner resources, placing appropriate resources in the appropriate relationship contexts. While the methodology employed does not provide a sound empirical test of this resource reshuffling hypothesis, the design and results do suggest its plausibility.

The results of this study need replication in order to further establish their reliability.

Appendix

The following is the written series of indirect suggestions read to the client. The italicized words and phrases were analogically marked (Lankton & Lankton, 1983) by changes in voice tone. Ellipses indicate brief pauses.

"Now the problem is this. You have not yet fully realized . . . in certain ways . . . that you can *use learnings, abilities, from one experience or several experiences . . . perhaps different in nature . . . in a problem situation.* You might use *comfort* from one experience . . . the ability *to forget* . . . the ability to *remember some things* while you *forget others* . . . the ability to *clearly state things in words* . . . the ability to *listen clearly,* as you can in one situation, and use the same ability in a situation where you might not consciously think you can . . . and other abilities from other experiences I haven't mentioned and don't even know. Imagine how a jigsaw puzzle that shows one scene might be made different by carefully replacing certain parts and pieces with different parts and pieces . . . an old picture made into a new one with old and new aspects. . . . Will your *unconscious do this now* and *change those old reactions to [D or H]* without you knowing consciously how your *unconscious will do it* . . . or would you rather tell me next time about surprisingly, newly *comfortable* and satisfying talks with [D or H] in those situations?

"Now what does your *unconscious think* that certain little girl in you can borrow from the adult in you so that when she sees . . . and hears . . . those things from [D or H] . . . and feels those old feelings . . . then she can *respond to those things differently, comfortably, satisfyingly, enjoyably . . .* you know, those things [D or H] does to get that little girl in you upset? What can your *unconscious* borrow from the adult in you so that *you will respond to those things in a surprisingly comfortable and enjoyable way*? What comfort can you use? . . . What adult abilities . . . the ability to talk . . . to *listen* . . . to *relax* . . . to forget . . . to remember . . . almost like the adult and little girl merge together in certain ways to *use old learning in new ways*. And what might *your unconscious* borrow from joyful, pleasant childhood experiences . . . the joy of *learning* . . . the pleasure of fun . . . the satisfaction of understanding . . . so many forgotten pleasant learnings that might be used in new ways . . . used in those situations with [D or H].

"How will *your unconscious now change the jigsaw puzzle of how you respond, think, feel, behave in those situations with [D or H]*? How can it replace old pieces with pieces and parts . . . abilities . . . from other childhood learnings of enjoyment and pleasure . . . to form a new and comfortably enjoyable response to [D or H]? What learnings will your *unconscious use in new ways* in those situations with [D or H]? What different things will you say? . . . *hear and understand* . . . perhaps things you haven't yet heard but have been there all along. . . . What experiences of comfort will your *unconscious* use so you *feel a certain comfort in those situations with [D or H]*? . . . How will *your unconscious* rearrange and restructure and alter and change and use learnings in new ways so that *from now on when you see those things* . . . *hear those things* . . . *you respond in a surprisingly pleasant and hard-to-believe comfortable way*?

"Would you rather consciously believe you will fail and be consciously surprised at how *your unconscious* alters the way you respond? . . . or would you rather just consciously wonder what will happen, without knowing how *your unconscious will change things so you respond in a pleasantly comfortable satisfying way in those situations with [D or H]*?

"Your *unconscious* can now *do everything necessary and possible and appropriate* . . . *in a manner fully meeting all your needs as a person* . . . *to insure that from now on with [D or H] you think, feel, speak, respond in satisfyingly pleasant and comfortable ways* during those situations . . . and as soon as your *unconscious* knows that you will *do these things*, then it can spontaneously awaken you from trance."

Notes

1. The IPA may not be familiar to readers unfamiliar with the social work literature. This scale has been in the literature since the late 1970s. The IPA has excellent known-groups validity, with the point-biserial correlation between IPA scores and clinician's assignment of clients to groups of distressed and nondistressed parent-child relationships of .88 (Hudson, 1982, p. 98). Hudson (1982, chapter 7) also reports evidence of construct and factorial validity for the IPA.

2. The IMS has been in the social work literature since the mid 1970s (see Hudson & Glisson, 1976). Hudson (1982, p. 98) reports a known-groups validity coefficient (i.e., the point-biserial correlation between IMS scores and membership in distressed or nondistressed marital groups) for the IMS of .82. Scores on the IMS also correlate very well with the Locke-Wallace Marital Adjustment Test (Corcoran & Fischer, 1987, p. 443), evidence for concurrent validity of the scale. Hudson (1982, chapter 7) also summarizes evidence for the construct and factorial validity of the IMS.

3. The author uses the metaphor of a jigsaw puzzle to represent Erickson's model of personal resources. The resources (experiences) are like pieces of a jigsaw puzzle, while the context the resources are imbedded in constitute the puzzle as a whole. The moving of resources from one context to another is likened to moving pieces of one jigsaw puzzle into a second puzzle (context). The prepared intervention used this metaphor to describe moving appropriate resources into the context of the woman's responses to provocative stimuli.

4. There have been few studies investigating the reliability and validity of retrospective measurements (see Bloom, 1963; Rippey et al., 1978). These studies have suggested retrospective data can be valid and reliable. However, given the paucity of evidence concerning the characteristics of retrospective data, it is best that it not be relied on to give an accurate indicator of preintervention levels of functioning (Bloom & Fischer, 1982; Campbell & Stanley, 1963). The study reported here uses both retrospective and concurrent baseline data. The concurrent baseline data should be used by the reader to ascertain preintervention levels of the target problem. The retrospective baselines give more qualitative indicators, consistent with verbal descriptions, of the historical stability of the client's interactional problems with daughter and husband.

References

Bloom, B. (1963). The thought process of students in discussion. In S. French (Ed.), *Accent on teaching* (pp. 23–46). New York: Harper & Row.

Bloom, M., & Fischer, J. (1982). *Evaluating practice*. Englewood Cliffs, NJ: Prentice-Hall.

Campbell, D., & Stanley, J. (1963). *Experimental and quasi-experimental designs for research*. Chicago: Rand-McNally.

Corcoran, K., & Fischer, J. (1987). *Measures for clinical practice*. New York: Free Press.

Erickson, M., & Rossi, E. (1979). *Hypnotherapy*. New York: Irvington.

Farkas, G., Sine, L., & Evans, I. (1979). The effects of distraction, performance demand, stimulus explicitness and personality on objective and subjective measures of male sexual arousal. *Behavior Research and Therapy, 17*, 25–32.

Fischer, J. (1978). *Effective casework practice*. New York: McGraw-Hill.

Gilligan, S. (1987). *Therapeutic trances.* New York: Brunner/Mazel.

Hudson, W. (1982). *The clinical measurement package.* New York: Dorsey.

Hudson, W., Wung, B., & Borges, M. (1980). Parent-child relationship disorders: The parent's point of view. *Journal of Social Service Research, 3,* 3.

Hudson, W., & Glisson, D. (1976). Assessment of marital discord in social work practice. *Social Service Review, 50,* 2.

Isaac, S., & Michael, W. (1971). *Handbook in research and evaluation.* San Diego, CA: Edits.

Kazdin, A. (1982). *Single case research designs.* New York: Oxford University Press.

Lankton, S., & Lankton, C. (1983). *The answer within.* New York: Brunner/Mazel.

Nugent, W. (1988a). A series of single case design clinical evaluations of an Ericksonian hypnotic intervention used with anxiety disorders. Manuscript under review.

Nugent, W. (1988b). A multiple baseline investigation of an Ericksonian hypnotic approach. *Ericksonian Monographs, 5,* 69–84.

Nugent, W. (1989a). Evidence concerning the causal effect of an Ericksonian hypnotic intervention. In S. R. Lankton (Ed.), *Ericksonian hypnosis: Application, preparation and research* (Ericksonian Monographs, 5, pp. 35–53). New York: Brunner/Mazel.

Nugent, W. (1989b). Psychometric characteristics of self-anchored scales in clinical application. *Journal of Social Service Research.*

Nugent, W., Carden, N., & Montgomery, D. (1984). Utilizing the creative unconscious in the treatment of hypodermic phobias and sleep disturbance. *American Journal of Clinical Hypnosis, 26,* 3, 201–205.

Patton, M. (1980). *Qualitative evaluation methods.* Beverly Hills, CA: Sage.

Rippey, R., Geller, L., & King, D. (1978). Retrospective pretesting in the cognitive domain. *Evaluation Quarterly, 2,* 481–491.

Thomas, E. (1978). Research and service in single case experimentation: Conflicts and choices. *Social Work Research and Abstracts, 14,* 20–31.

Thyer, B., Papsdorf, J., Davis, R. & Vallecorsa, S. (1984). Autonomic correlates of the subjective anxiety scale. *Journal of Behavior Therapy and Experimental Psychiatry, 15,* 1, 3–7.

Wincze, J., Hoon, P., & Hoon, E. (1977). Sexual arousal in women: A comparison of cognitive and physiological responses by continuous measurement. *Archives of Sexual Behavior, 6,* 121–133.

The Art of Examining a Child: Use of Naturalistic Methods in the Pediatric Physical Examination

John C. Gall, M.D.

A number of specific procedures are presented for facilitating the pediatric physical examination. These are based on established hypnotic methods, specifically: confusion, polarity, yes-set, lacuna, implication, utilization, engineered spontaneity, choices, guided fantasy, and frame-of-reference management. By means of procedures based on those methods, an infant, toddler, or older child can be maintained in a state of comfort and relaxed attention of sufficient duration to permit the attainment of the goals of the pediatric physical examination, including blood pressure measurement, throat swabbing for cultures, and even injections for immunizations. Respect for the child's physical and mental integrity and for the child's view of the world are stressed as fundamental principles for successful and therapeutic interaction with the child.

Since the publication of Milton H. Erickson's pioneering paper, "Pediatric Hypnotherapy" (1958), the value of hypnotic approaches in alleviation of certain types of pediatric problems has been increasingly recognized, and the use of such methods has increased significantly in recent years (Gardner, 1977; Gardner & Olness, 1981; Kohen et al., 1984). However, less attention has been paid to the application of hypnosis and

Some of the material in this paper was presented in a talk given at the Second Annual Spring Conference of the Milton H. Erickson Institute of Michigan on April 9, 1988. The author is Clinical Associate Professor in the Department of Pediatrics and Communicable Diseases, University of Michigan Medical School, and is in full-time private practice of pediatrics in Ann Arbor. The work on which this paper was based was derived from private practice experience and was not supported in whole or in part by grant funds. Address correspondence to: John Gall, M.D., 3200 West Liberty Road, Ann Arbor, MI 48103-9794.

related approaches to the actual examination of infants and children by the pediatrician. Specific hints or instructions to the pediatrician as to how to go about using such methods on a day-to-day basis are occasionally encountered (cf. Baumann, 1982), but such hints are typically scattered, often in the form of incidental or informal remarks, and often referred to vaguely as part of the "art of medicine." The purpose of the present paper is to present a number of such methods collected by the author over a number of years in private practice of pediatrics. It is hoped that their presentation in one place, in a format that emphasizes their relevance to the pragmatic goals of the clinician, will encourage others to give them a try, to keep those that are useful, and hopefully to develop still more methods that will provide increased elegance to the art of the pediatric examination.

The Comfort State in Pediatrics

The clinician's concern is the elicitation of a state of comfort and relaxed attention in which the pediatric examination can be carried out without resistance, agitation, or fear—not necessarily the production of deep trance. There is usually no advantage in a formal hypnotic induction under such circumstances. As Erickson (1958) has stated, "There is seldom, if ever, a need for a formalized or ritualistic technique" in dealing with children (p. 29). Indeed, it is better to elicit a number of brief moments of relaxed attention and comfort, during which procedures may be deftly performed, than try for a formal deep trance, which may be unsuccessful and result in loss of rapport and possibly cause active resistance to further examination.

Thus, most of the approaches reported herein are "naturalistic" in the Ericksonian sense. They appear simply as the normal and natural behavior of a competent clinician going about his or her task. The mother of an infant may be pleased that her 8-month-old has taken a shine to the examiner but will not necessarily realize that the baby's smile was deliberately induced by forehead-approximation. Similarly, the parents of a 5-year-old may watch him "helping" the examiner "test" the otoscope without realizing that the examiner is at that very moment examining the child's ears.

An infant who is in a comfortable frame of reference doesn't have to be held down to be examined. He or she smiles when you touch the back of the tongue with the tongue blade and trigger off the gag reflex. He or she thinks that's amusing and lets you do it again and again just to experience the curious pleasure of feeling the gag reflex working over and over. A toddler who is in a comfort frame doesn't regard the ophthalmoscope light as scary or painful, but stares right back at it and smiles. The frame of reference is not that of "being examined," but rather that of having fun with the doctor and with the doctor's toys. And the otoscope speculum tickling the auditory canal is nothing terrible; it's not an invasion of the body; it's just a very interesting tickling feeling in the ear.

There is no set, limited number of ways of inducing a state of relaxed attention in a child, or in anyone else for that matter. There are as many ways as there are ways of interacting with people. The methods suggested in this paper merely represent some of the ways that have been found by one clinician to succeed often enough to be worth mastering and using regularly. Sensitivity to feedback (i.e., awareness of the patient's responses) is essential and can be substantially improved by study of the spontaneous response repertoire of infants and children (Givens, 1978). In the long run, the clinician who masters a repertoire of such methods will almost certainly experience a quantum leap of personal satisfaction in professional practice.

The overall effect of such an approach in the examination setting is therapeutic in at least three ways: 1) by replacing the traditional "painful" frame of reference applied to the doctor's office with one of comfort, trust, positive interest, and actual pleasure; 2) by modeling for the parent(s) how to interact with a child in such a way as to promote comfort, trust and a sense of competence; and 3) by providing the child with an actual experience of such an interaction.

Parental Involvement

The correct diagnosis of tight and highly charged linkages between parent and infant is one of the most important tasks of the so-called well-baby examination, or indeed of the sick-baby examination, and is a prerequisite for success in the practice of pediatrics. In general, any interaction with a child that is undertaken without reference to the ongoing relationship between the parent(s) and the infant, and between the parent(s) and the examiner, is likely to encounter unexpected responses (Gardner, 1974). The infant who is at the moment functioning as the sounding board for parental anxiety or other emotions is not free to respond to the examiner in the same way as an infant more loosely linked to the parental presence. The examiner may decide that the first step is to create a state of comfort and nonperformance in the parent(s). Then the way is more likely to be clear for achieving the pragmatic goals of the examination of the infant.

Parental expectations of trouble are "telegraphed" to the infant or toddler by nonverbal as well as by verbal means. For example, when weighing an infant on the baby scale, the parent who hovers close after placing the infant on the scale is figuratively inviting the infant to clutch for the parent and scream to be removed. To prevent this outcome, the parent can be invited to put the baby on the scale and then step backward four steps.

The Utilization Approach in the Examination of the Infant

The utilization approach, pioneered by Erickson (1959), is of major importance in the examination of children and especially of tiny infants. The basic idea is simple. If the infant yawns, one utilizes that opportunity to examine the infant's mouth. In other words, the spontaneous behavior of the infant is utilized when it occurs. The method can be carried one step further, in that spontaneous behavior can be actively triggered or elicited by the examiner. The infant's eyes, for example, can be caused to pop open by the simple expedient of turning off the overhead lights.

What often happens in the standard pediatric examination of the infant will be recognized by many practitioners as a comedy of errors in which the examiner, preparing to examine the next item on his or her mental list, inadvertently triggers the exact defensive reaction that renders that particular examination difficult or impossible. For example, an attempt to pry open the infant's mouth with a tongue blade produces vigorous clamping of the lips and gums. Utilization may thus be thought of as the opposite of the standard approach to the examination of the infant.

Spontaneous mouth opening, to continue this example, can be elicited by any one of a number of maneuvers. In the neonate, stroking the lower lip with the examiner's knuckle is often sufficient. While maintaining this contact, the tongue blade is quickly inserted, touching the tongue only at the most posterior region. Under such circumstances, the tongue blade is often reacted to as if it were food. Defensive tongue movements are not elicited. The resulting gag-swallow, which occurs reflexly, is usually experienced by the infant not as a threat but as part of the sequence of swallowing a mouthful of milk.

Alternatively, advantage can be taken of the reflexive mouth opening that tends to occur when the infant's eyes try to follow a moving object upward past the horizontal. Playfully "walking" the examiner's fingers upward from navel to lower lip may produce the same result. Some infants respond to forehead-approach with a gaping grin, which can be utilized to examine the throat.

Methods of Physical Approach to the Infant

Proximity, especially to strangers, is a major concern for babies, as it is for everyone. The actual moment of physical approach toward the infant is therefore critical. If anxiety is triggered, it may be difficult to gain rapport.

Tope Borrego

The method of approach must be compatible with the developmental level of the infant or child. A method that is applicable over a wide range of developmental levels is a slow, smiling approximation of the examiner's face to the infant's face, culminating in a gentle, playful approximation of forehead to forehead. This is commonly recognized by infants beyond the newborn stage as a playful game. Many mothers spontaneously discover or invent this game on their own. In Latin cultures it is sufficiently well known to have a special name, *tope borrego*, or lamb's butt (cf. mutual gaze or *en face* position, Givens, 1978).

Head approach is most effective when the infant is either prone or in the sitting position, since the infant in these positions has some control over head position and can tilt the head forward and downward to participate. In the supine position the maneuver may be experienced as threatening, particularly if the examiner approaches from above, since the infant essentially cannot move the head to participate. With the infant in supine position, the success rate is higher if the examiner approaches from one side, with the examiner's head at about the same level as the infant's.

Whether or not the examiner uses forehead-approach, a method that avoids approach from above is less likely to be threatening. For example, when auscultating the infant's chest, the examiner stands at the foot of the table and moves the stethoscope cephalad past the (supine) infant's feet and abdomen to reach the chest. The stethoscope need never enter the infant's field of vision. The probability of a defensive reaction is thus minimized.

For the infant or toddler who consistently looks away from the examiner or who appears anxious on face-approach, the examiner can approach forehead-to-occiput, gradually working forward as the child exhibits signs of increasing security and pleasure in the game.

Slow-Down or "Freeze-Frame" Approach

A second method, closely related to the first, which can be employed either separately or in conjunction with it, is the "slow-down" approach, in which the examiner slows down his or her gestures by a factor of two or three or more, in effect going into "slow motion." The infant will often respond immediately by defocusing eyes, staring into space or into the examiner's eyes (only a few inches from his or her own), and exhibiting either a slight smile or a slack, solemn, relaxed facial expression with or without associated drooling. Infants in sitting position often exhibit a sudden loss of truncal control at this time, with resulting sudden lurch forward.

The slow-down can be carried all the way to a "freeze-frame" if necessary, in order to intensify the fixation and further distance the child from usual consciousness. An infant or toddler lying supine on the examining table can be maintained in such a state with the cooperation of the parents, who stand immobile and stare into space above the child's head.

Peek-a-Boo Approach

Still another method, useful for the infant old enough to sit up or for the young toddler, is the peek-a-boo approach, in which the child's chart or a large card is held in front of the examiner's face. The examiner peeks out from one side or the other while gradually moving closer. With infants lying supine the infant's shirt can be used as a prop. Engaged in playing peek-a-boo with the shirt tail, the infant may fail to notice the stethoscope placed on its chest.

Mock-Threat Approach

For a certain type of toddler who likes adventure, there is the mock-threat approach: "I'm gonna get you!" This can be combined at times with a mock pursuit. This approach can be considered as a specific counter to stranger anxiety; it tends to evoke a frame of reference that excludes stranger anxiety reactions or fearfulness. Mock fear on the examiner's part may produce the same effect.

Nonverbal Confusion Technique

If both cheeks are gently grasped at once with thumb and third finger, respectively, while the infant or toddler is in sitting position or supine, the child will often not know which way to resist and will do nothing; the child will go into a trance-like state, easily detectable by the defocusing of the eyes. The effect can be heightened by alternately pressing on one cheek and then the other, and by varying the pressure while diminishing it to the point of undetectability (cf. Erickson, 1964a). The hand can then be removed with persistence of the trance-like state.

Another method of nonverbal induction of a confusion state is as follows: With an infant old enough to sit without assistance, place one hand behind the head and gently push forward while simultaneously lifting with the other hand placed under the infant's thighs. The infant will not know which push to resist and, having no agenda, may go into a trance-like state. This maneuver often permits the examiner to place the infant in the supine position without resistance and with concomitant production of a comfort frame.

Initial Framing in the Approach to the Toddler or Older Child

Cookie-Eater Frame

The examiner can take control of the framing process at the outset by moving into the waiting room entrance and announcing: "Angela! You just came here to eat my cookies again, didn't you?" or "You just came here to play with my toys." If the response to this opening gambit is one of amusement or even enthusiasm, the examiner can continue the conversation along the same lines as the child enters the examining room.

Little Big Person, or Authority Frame

A first-grader or kindergartner can be given authority by saying, "Bring your Mom. Tell her she has to come with you. Tell here where she has to sit. Show her where *you* are going to sit." The reversal of roles is often eagerly seized upon by the child with a smile of complicity that reveals that (at some level of awareness) she or he knows what's going on.

The Yes-Set (Erickson, 1964b)

For appropriately responsive toddlers, preschoolers and school-age children, the yes-set is one of the quickest ways of inducing compliant (trance-like) behavior. The child is approached in the waiting room with questions to which the only possible answer is "yes." For example: "Is that you, Jennifer? Are you here today? Did you come here with your mother today? Are you walking with your mother now? Are you walking into my room?"

This sequence of questions rapidly induces a state in which the child is already beginning to answer "yes" even as the question is being asked. The usual indicators of trance can be observed as a check on the effectiveness of the approach: The child will begin to move rather slowly and automatically; the face will become somewhat slack and expressionless; the "yes" responses will become nearly identical in intonation; and the child will give evidence of inattention to surroundings other than those marked out by the examiner.

As the child enters the room, the questions continue: "Are you getting up on my table? Are you sitting on the table? Are you looking up at the light?" With this approach a complete examination can be carried out, often with some degree of amnesia for the event on the part of the child. (A hand signal can be used to caution the mother or father to remain silent and motionless.)

Preempting or Dissipating Resistance

By actively initiating a suitable frame of reference (as above), the examiner can often preempt resistant behavior. On the other hand, a child who is already prepared to resist examination to the utmost can be approached while still riding the wooden rocking horse in the waiting room. The examiner may be able to check ears, etc., while the child is still on the horse. After all, if one is not even in the examining room, it can't be an examination, can it? The child may go home believing that he or she was not really examined at all. Or a toddler who is investing all his or her energy in resisting the idea of the *doctor's* examination may have no resistance left over for the nurse practitioner, who may carry out part or all of the examination while assuring the toddler that she won't let the doctor come near.

The toddler who announces loudly while still in the waiting room that he or she definitely does not want to go into the doctor's examining room, does not want to be examined by the doctor, does not want to get down out of mother's arms, can be informed in a strong and authoritative voice, "You don't want to go in that room. You don't want to be examined. You don't want to get down. You want to stay in your mommy's arms." The mere act of verbal recognition of the child's position (verbal pacing) is often enough to produce a double-take with sudden reversal of attitude which permits further development of rapport.

On the other hand, an infant or child who is asleep in the mother's arms can be examined almost completely while still asleep, if proper caution is observed.

In general, achieving a satisfactory level of success with such interventions depends upon being at all times keenly aware of whether a given intervention is working, and being ready to shift quickly and unobtrusively to another approach when necessary.

Approaches for Giving Injections

With appropriate technique, a clinician should be able to give an injection intramuscularly to a 3-month-old infant without triggering crying on about 50% of occasions. If crying does occur, the clinician should know several ways to limit or interrupt it, with return to the preimmunization level of comfort. With some older children, the injection can be given in such a way that the child is not sure whether it was given or not, or in which leg it was given, if it was given. Older children whose mental set is that they know quite well what shots are can have the experience of getting an injection that is *less painful* than expected.

Infants

Certain sounds are especially interesting to infants. Rushing water or rattling paper has powerful distracting qualities. An intramuscular injection given in the anterior thigh can actually be ignored by an infant engrossed in a piece of rattling paper held near its face (cf. Gardner, 1977). Bells and music boxes, objects that click repetitively, and simple toys that make a grinding or machine-like noise have similar powers.

Visual displays that have compelling properties include mobiles, especially if they move back and forth with a pendulum-like motion. A doll or figurine suspended on an elastic band from the ceiling is especially engrossing to infants old enough to reach and grasp. The experience of power and control involved in making the doll bounce against the ceiling is highly gratifying to many infants at that age and stage of development.

The distracting power of such sights and sounds can be enhanced by incorporating them into the sequence known as the *associative gap* or *lacuna* method (Erickson et al., 1959; Erickson & Rossi, 1979). An infant who is busily trying to reach for a dangling key, a bright plastic toy, or a bottle held almost within reach by the parent may not notice the twinge as an injection is given into the anterior thigh (Gardner, 1977), particularly if the examiner stays out of the infant's visual field. If the twinge is noticed, the key, toy or bottle may be held a bit closer and the infant resumes the attempt to attain the fascinating, elusive goal.

For infants too young to reach for objects, the lacuna technique can be employed in conjunction with face-approach or forehead-approximation. As the infant becomes entrained in the delights of repeated face-approximation, one such sequence is interrupted by the injection, with immediate resumption of the sequence. The twinge may be barely noticed and immediately forgotten. Some infants go into a trance-like state with repeated face-approach and the injection appears to produce no pain response, nor indeed any response at all.

An infant or young child crying vigorously from an injection may stop crying instantly on being carried through the doorway of the examining room. A return to the doorway or even to its vicinity may promptly elicit a recurrence of the crying at the same level of intensity as when it was interrupted, clearly indicating the sudden shift of ego state involved in the lacuna method. Because of this effect, the infant who has just received an injection should not be returned to the examining table where the injection was just given. "Getting away" is a scenario that is understood at a deep visceral level by tiny infants as well as by adults.

Toddlers

For a toddler at the peak of stranger anxiety (around 15–24 months) a modified lacuna method can be employed: The injection is prepared in advance and, with the cooperation of the parents, is given so swiftly (less than 10 seconds) that the entire procedure is over and the child is back in the playroom in too short a time to develop a fear reaction.

Older Children

For older children, establishing the correct frame of reference at the outset is important, as was discussed earlier. Much unnecessary suffering and apprehension are caused by parents and doctors habitually operating within a certain frame of reference, thereby establishing a repeating pattern in pediatric practice that could be called "going to the doctor and getting hurt." The well-child checkup or annual physical examination is equated with "getting your shots," when it could equally well have the experience value implied by "getting the green form filled out so you can go to school" or "going to play with the doctor's toys."

An older child can be invited into a formal trance by the suggestion, "You can raise your arm over your head and have a nice dream. And you can *try* to keep your eyes open as you keep on dreaming" (Erickson & Rossi, 1981; Grinder & Bandler, 1981). A variation is the multiple-task approach, in which the child can be asked, for example, to bring the thumbs together so they are just barely touching, then to keep them touching while sticking out the tongue as far as possible, then to roll the eyes upward while maintaining thumb touching and tongue extension. The multiplicity of tasks ties up conscious attention, leaving little attention available for anxiety. A child who is asked at this point, "Will you wait for me like that?" may go into a trance-like state that permits the completion of several parts of the physical examination or the perform- ance of procedures such as immunization or swabbing the throat for culture of organisms. "And when I look in your ear, be sure to stick your tongue out as far as possible."

The child who does not readily go into a formal trance can be invited to use an ice cube on the thigh as a numbing method, both before and after the injection, thereby making use of the lacuna method as well as the direct power of suggestion. The objectively demonstrable numbing power of ice adds powerfully to its placebo effect. Or the examiner may search with a fingernail for tiny "numb spots" on the skin surface. Careful placement of the needle into a "numb spot" previously identified as such by the child may result in complete anesthesia for the injection. As an aid to amnesia for the whole event, the child can be advised (once only!) to "skip it" or "forget it."

Further Methods in Examination of
Toddlers and Older Children

Engineered Spontaneity, Guided Fantasy

Most babies, toddlers, and preschoolers don't usually like to "perform." If you ask them to do something that you know they can do, something that you have seen them do—indeed, something that they have just done and done with enjoyment—they won't do it. It's a matter of principle and they are prepared to resist you to the bitter end. So you don't ask them. Instead, you just set things up so that they *spontaneously* feel the impulse to do it. (Cf. *"protohypnosis,* in which the distraction has at first been set up in the external situation," Hilgard & Morgan 1978, p. 286, cited in Gardner & Olness, 1981, p. 33).

Example. A carved wooden seagull hangs from the ceiling of the examination room, delicately poised in mid-flight. A seashell hangs from a string attached to the bird. It's just high enough that a 3-year-old can pull the footstool up under the mobile and stand erect, looking upward, to reach the seashell and pull the bird into motion, causing the wings to flap gently and slowly.

As the child stands on the stool, balances, and reaches upward, cerebellar function and hand-eye coordination are prominently displayed. Impulsivity and/or hyperactivity can be assessed from the way the child performs the whole sequence. The status of the child's cervical lymph nodes can be assessed visually and by palpation almost without the child's noticing. The mouth will often fall open spontaneously or in response to a whispered request while the head is thus tilted upward. The tympanic membranes can be inspected with ease.

The entire apparatus serves the purpose of permitting the examiner to make certain assessments while the child is absorbed in doing something of great interest to the child. Utilization of such engineered "spontaneous" behavior is the essence of the method. The actual mobile is, of course, not essential. It is only a prop. The same outcome can be achieved by means of appropriate suggestions: "Do you see that cricket up there in the ceiling light? There, up there in the ceiling. See? Up there. Can you see where he's hiding?"

Parents may be so concerned about possible damage to the apparatus that they may not realize that the child was actually examined. In such cases, it is advisable to point out to the parents what "actually" happened, so that they will not think the examiner incompetent.

Getting a 2-year-old to take deep breaths for auscultation of the chest is often difficult. Children this age sometimes seem to become paralyzed by the effort to do voluntarily what is ordinarily an unconscious, spontaneous process. But if they have already enthusiastically mastered the art of sticking out their tongue and saying, "Ah-h-h," while looking up at the ceiling and keeping their thumbs stuck together, they can be asked again to say, "Ah-h-h," and the subsequent irresistible need to inhale will meet the examiner's needs quite well.

As a further example of engineered "spontaneity," a child can be informed that the examiner's flashlight hasn't been working well recently.

Might the examiner test it by shining it here, there? "Will you help me test it? Will it shine bright enough to see your mouth, your tongue, your tonsils, your ears? Will you take the batteries out and see if they're OK?" (while examiner checks heart and lungs with the stethoscope).

Engineered "spontaneity" of this type merges into the approach called *guided fantasy*, in which the child is encouraged to have a fantasy experience, of which certain features are suggested by the examiner (Satir, 1972). A special case of guided fantasy is the use of a stuffed toy. The child who brings a stuffed toy or an imaginary playmate into the examining room, or who accepts a proffered stuffed toy from the examiner, is indicating a readiness to join the examiner in entering a magical world where the experiences of the child can merge with those of the toy or imaginary playmate. A physical examination can be carried out on the teddy bear simultaneously with that of the child. The child can admonish Teddy, "Now, hold your ear still!" even as the examiner is inspecting the child's tympanic membranes.

Choices

Once in the examining room, the child can be asked, "Do *you* want to tell me about it or do you want Mom (or Dad) to tell me?" The vast majority of children this age indicate they want Mom or Dad to tell about it. But they have been asked! They have been respected. They have been given the authority to make a decision about themselves. And no matter what their decision is, the examiner still gets the history of the present illness.

Polarity; the No-Set; Getting the Better of the Doctor

The toddler who is beginning to develop a sense of autonomy and self-identity by saying "No!" to almost everything and by exhibiting other forms of oppositional behavior can be commanded: *"Don't* pull up your shirt!" If the examiner senses a certain amount of anxiety about the proceedings, a slightly more complex command can be issued: "Hold your shirt *down* in front!"—while the examiner auscultates the *posterior* chest. Some children are comfortable holding the shirt *down* in front but slightly away from the body while the examiner auscultates the heart. They are willing for the examiner to succeed if they, too, are allowed to succeed (in holding the shirt *down*).

This *polarity strategy* or reverse-set double-bind (Erickson et al., 1976) can be combined with an implicit appeal to the delightful sense of triumph in accomplishment, especially if one of the accomplishments is to (apparently) frustrate the doctor and/or the child's parents and show them a thing or two. Thus: "You couldn't climb up on that table, could you? It's too high for you!" A typical response is, "Oh, yes, I can. See!"—accompanied by an energetic and triumphant performance of the challenge. This can be followed up by a wondering question, "Do you know how to pull up your own shirt . . . in the front *and* in the back?"—accompanied by appropriate expressions of pleased surprise.

The Confusion Approach

The confusion approach (Erickson, 1964c) can be considered as being located conceptually somewhere about halfway between the polarity strategy and the yes-set. It occupies the middle ground. The child does not know whether to comply or to resist and typically does nothing, that is, exhibits trance-like behavior. Confusion can be initiated by speaking to the "wrong" child (of two or more), asking the first child to open the mouth, for example, while actually looking into the other child's mouth (cf. Baumann, 1982).

A preschool child who has proudly marched up and stood on the scale may be allowed to stand there without further instructions while another sibling is dealt with. If the child continues to stand motionless on the scale, the trance-like state can be employed to carry out further portions of the examination. The trance-like state can be deepened by the indefinite request, "Will you wait for me?" A slow affirmative head-nodding or a whispered "Yes" will allow the examiner to spend some time discussing findings with the parent(s), confident that the child will continue to stand quietly on the scale.

A child who is sitting on the examining table can be asked, "Can you lean back and look up at the mobile so I can count your toes?" It's difficult for a child to object to someone counting their toes. The fact that you are at that moment palpating their spleen is likely to be overlooked, as they are too busy imagining you counting their toes.

The yes-set and the polarity response can be alternately elicited in such a way that the toddler feels that the interactions are entirely spontaneous: "Does your tongue stick out when you open your mouth? Can you keep it in with your mouth open?"

Requests of this type merge into more paradoxical communications such as, "Open your nose!" The toddler confronted with such a command will often open the mouth in a trance-like state because of the impossibility of making sense of the order as given. She or he "goes inside" and searches for some other command, resembling the one just given, that *does* make sense. If the examiner is touching the toddler's lower lip at that moment, the implied directive given by the touch may cause the command to be translated into "Open your mouth!" But since no such order was given verbally, the toddler may find *nothing to resist*.

Younger toddlers, who have not yet learned the limitations of "reality," often respond with a truly amazing flare of the nostrils. This "success" at opening the nose can be carried over to opening the eyes, the ears, the mouth.

"Where's your chewing gum?" (and subsequent search for the nonexistent gum in the triumphantly opened mouth) avoids the entire issue of opening the mouth for the examiner. The child is not "opening his or her mouth," but achieving the personal goal of triumphing over the examiner by showing that there is no gum . . . anywhere.

"Is your tongue green?" accomplishes the same goal. "What about the back part of it? Is that part green? Is it really pink all the way back?" A child who responds with reluctance to the request, "May I see your tongue?" may respond with enthusiasm to the request "Can you show me your teeth?" The act (opening the jaws) is the same, but the implications are different.

Simultaneous Rapport

Establishing simultaneous rapport seems less formidable if one realizes that it is something that everyone does to some extent. At home, we relate differently to our spouse if a child is present in the room. Multiple simultaneous verbal and nonverbal communications can be used deliberately to establish rapport with the infant or child to be examined even while one is making contact with the parent. A quick tongue-thrust or eye-pop directed toward the infant serves to alert him or her that further communication can be expected. The child or infant then goes into the mental state that can be designated as "expectancy of communication" or "rapport," characterized by heightened attentiveness to the examiner and diminished attention to the rest of the environment. The parent(s) may not even notice (at least consciously) that you are sticking out your tongue at the baby while talking to the parent(s) about the symptoms. Baby does not notice that you are talking to Mom while sticking out your tongue at Baby. Each is in rapport only with that part of your communication that is aimed at them specifically and individually (mutual trance induction; Erickson et al., 1976).

A special case of simultaneous rapport is the simultaneous examination of siblings. Sibling rivalry and competitiveness usually provide strong motivation for this maneuver. The siblings can be invited or induced to sit or lie side by side on the examining table. The older, more sophisticated sibling may be examined first. This procedure often induces unconscious or even deliberate imitation on the part of the younger sibling, who will open his or her mouth even wider to prove she or he is just as good as brother or sister. If the younger sibling is a toddler, one can use sibling rivalry to enlist the active demand of the younger sibling for equal time and attention. A variation that is useful when one sibling is an infant is to invite the older sibling to stand on a low stool and "supervise" the examination of the infant.

"Stretching the Umbilical Cord" (Using Spatial Distancing from the Parent)

The examiner (or the parent) can utilize the ambivalence of the toddler about being separated from the parent(s) to get him or her to move closer or farther away according to the specific desired results.

Stretching the umbilical cord can also be combined with the natural polarity response of this stage to structure a rather powerful motivation to move in a certain direction. A toddler can even be invited to leave shoes and socks off and continue to play in the doctor's office because he or she "doesn't have to" go home with the parents right now. This maneuver often results in a hasty insistence on getting dressed and going with the parents.

Implication

"Now, I don't want you climbing up on my table until I say so, OK?" The *implication* is that this activity is both fun and forbidden. The humorous outrageousness of the request *implies* that the doctor wouldn't really object too much if it were disobeyed. The child has the opportunity to disobey an authority figure and carry out a forbidden act that might even be fun. On the other hand, if she or he decides to wait until the doctor says so, the child is still doing what the doctor wants. Either way, the child gets to decide, and either way, the doctor gets a satisfactory outcome. The hidden implication in the statement is the idea that the child *will* eventually climb up on the table (implied directive; Erickson et al., 1976).

"Next time you come here . . ." This casual remark takes for granted the inevitability of another visit sometime in the future and thus preempts a future surprise and the turmoil of negative feelings that often accompany surprise.

A special form of verbal implication is the imbedded command: "Do you know how to *take off your shoes and throw them on the floor*? And can you *throw your socks so they fall right on your shoes*?" "Now when you get home with your medicine, I want you to take it and put it in the refrigerator and hide it behind the pickles, where nobody else can find it, because it's all yours and nobody else gets to drink any of it. And remember, only one spoonful!"

The repertoire of *nonverbal* implication techniques is vast, constituting a complete language antedating verbal communication and of substantially greater power, particularly since nonverbal communication tends to be understood at an unconscious level. The very act of paying attention to one thing rather than another tends to shape the other person's picture of the world by indicating that some things are more worthy of attention than others. One's dress, body posture, gestures, speed of movement and response, and voice tonality are components of nonverbal communication. As nonverbal implication is an implicit part of most of the techniques described in this paper, no attempt will be made to treat it as a separate topic. In general, for purposes of the pediatric examination, nonverbal communication should convey the implications, "I respect and care for you" and "This is play."

Discussion

The basic principle underlying the naturalistic approach to the examination of the child is respect for the integrity of the child—both mental and physical integrity—and for the child's view of the world. Naturally, the child's view of the world is different from that of adults. The essence of the naturalistic approach is to pace into the *child's* view, rather than trying to force the adult's view onto the child. As Erickson has said:

> No matter what the age of the child may be, there should never be any threat to the child as a functioning unit of society. Adult physical strength, intellectual strength, force of authority, and weight of prestige are all so immeasurably greater to the child than his own attributes that any undue use constitutes a threat to his adequacy as an individual. (1958, p. 26)

Children who have experienced this type of enlightened approach recognize that their individuality, their dignity, and their need for comfortable interaction with the world have been respected, and their later behavior reflects this understanding. At the toddler stage it is typically manifested by a kind of compulsion to return to the examining room while the parents are occupied at the front office. On return visits, there may be an enthusiastic dash to get into the examining room—even to climb up on the table. Parents will often report that the child has made remarks from time to time at home indicating interest, curiosity, and pleasure in connection with the previous medical examination. The examiner is justified in accepting these signs of satisfaction as indications of the success of his or her technique in the examination of the child.

References

Baumann, F. (1982). Hypnotherapy with children and adolescents: Some Ericksonian ideas. In J. K. Zeig (Ed.), *Ericksonian approaches to hypnosis and psychotherapy.* New York: Brunner/Mazel.

Erickson, M. H. (1958). Pediatric hypnotherapy. *The American Journal of Clinical Hypnosis, 1,* 25–29.

Erickson, M. H. (1959). Further techniques of hypnosis—utilization techniques. *The American Journal of Clinical Hypnosis, 2,* 3–21.

Erickson, M. H. (1964a). Pantomime techniques in hypnosis and the implications. *The American Journal of Clinical Hypnosis, 7,* 65–70.

Erickson, M. H. (1964b). A hypnotic technique for resistant patients. *The American Journal of Clinical Hypnosis, 7,* 152–162.

Erickson, M. H. (1964c). The confusion technique in hypnosis. *The American Journal of Clinical Hypnosis, 6,* 183–207.

Erickson, M. H., Haley, J., & Weakland, J. (1959). A transcript of a trance induction with commentary. *American Journal of Clinical Hypnosis, 2,* 49–84.

Erickson, M. H., Rossi, E. L., & Rossi, S. I. (1976). *Hypnotic realities. The induction of clinical hypnosis and forms of indirect suggestion.* New York: Irvington.

Erickson, M. H., & Rossi, E. L. (1979). *Hypnotherapy: An exploratory casebook.* New York: Irvington.

Erickson, M. H., & Rossi, E. L. (1981). *Experiencing hypnosis: Therapeutic approaches to altered states.* New York: Irvington.

Gardner, G. G. (1974). Parents: Obstacles or allies in child hypnotherapy? *The American Journal of Clinical Hypnosis, 17,* 44–49.

Gardner, G. G. (1977). Hypnosis with infants and preschool children. *The American Journal of Clinical Hypnosis, 19,* 158–162.

Gardner, G. G., & Olness, K. N. (1981). *Hypnosis and hypnotherapy with children.* New York: Grune & Stratton.

Givens, D. (1978). Social expressivity during the first year of life. *Sign Language Studies, 20,* 251–274.

Grinder, J., & Bandler, R. (1981). *Trance-formations, neuro-linguistic programming and the structure of hypnosis.* Moab, UT: Real People Press.

Hilgard, J. R., & Morgan, A. H. (1978). Treatment of anxiety and pain in childhood cancer through hypnosis. In F. H. Frankel & H. S. Zamansky (Eds.). *Hypnosis at its bicentennial: Selected papers.* New York: Plenum Press.

Kohen, D. P., Olness, K. N., Colwell, S. O., et al. (1984). The use of relaxation mental imagery (self-hypnosis) in the management of 505 pediatric behavioral encounters. *Journal of Developmental and Behavioral Pediatrics, 5,* 1.

Satir, V. (1972). *Peoplemaking.* Palo Alto, CA: Science & Behavior Books.